"When I read Rolf's book, *The Family Blessing*, I knew immediately that he was addressing one of the most important issues our families face today. I recommend that everyone interested in sharing God's goodness and favor with others read this book again and again."
ZIG ZIGLAR
author and motivational teacher

"If you can read this without a lump in your throat, there's something wrong with your throat."
JERRY B. JENKINS
co-author of the New York Times bestselling Left Behind series

"You have to be blessed to be a blessing to others. Rolf's cup overflows with blessings. Be ye contagious."
MARK VICTOR HANSEN
co-creator of the New York Times bestselling Chicken Soup for the Soul series

"As Rolf Garborg shows...nothing is wiser than learning His way of transmitting His blessing from generation to generation."
JACK W. HAYFORD
founding pastor/chancellor, The Church on the Way, The King's College and Seminary, Van Nuys, CA

"Every night, as we tuck our six children into bed, we are asked, 'Can I have my blessing now?' As our babies grow up into young adults, they are continually reminded by their family blessing that they are loved by God, delighted in by their parents, and have a rich future awaiting them as followers of Christ. The tradition of a 'family blessing' as Rolf shares in this book has become a priceless and vital part of our daily lives."
KIRK AND CHELSEA CAMERON
co-stars of nationally syndicated hit *Growing Pains*

Group resources really work!

This Group resource incorporates our R.E.A.L. approach to ministry. It reinforces a growing friendship with Jesus, encourages long-term learning, and results in life transformation, because it's

Relational
Learner-to-learner interaction enhances learning and builds Christian friendships.

Experiential
What learners experience through discussion and action sticks with them up to 9 times longer than what they simply hear or read.

Applicable
The aim of Christian education is to equip learners to be both hearers and doers of God's Word.

Learner-based
Learners understand and retain more when the learning process takes into consideration how they learn best.

THE FAMILY
BLESSING

ROLF GARBORG

_To_

From

Date

CONTENTS

Sections of Special Interest

Several years ago, our girls were settling into bed after a delightful evening of "family week" activities at our church. We had just watched the film entitled *The Blessing*, featuring Gary Smalley and John Trent, and I could tell that the bedtime prayer for my ten- and seven-year-old daughters would be shaped by this new perspective. The film had left me with overwhelming feelings of inadequacy as I pondered my calling, my responsibility, and my deep longing as a father to be a blessing to my children.

As a pastor, I was accustomed to pronouncing "benedictions," but not until that moment in the spring of 1991 had I considered pronouncing a benediction over my children. Not until that moment had these girls felt their daddy's right hand on their heads while he called upon the God of Abraham, Isaac, and Jacob to bless them. Not until that moment had I felt such assurance from my heavenly Father that He would be for my daughters a blessing of infinite value beyond all that I could hope to be. Not until that moment had I, with such earnest and desperate desire, looked into the eyes of each daughter and said:

May the *Lord* bless you and keep you!
May the *Lord* make His face shine on you and be
    gracious to you!
May the *Lord* lift up His countenance on you and give
    you peace!

In that moment, a new element was added to our bedtime routine that brought over the next decade many cherished and unforgettable moments with the Lord and my children.

A few months after our first bedtime blessing, I read the first edition of *The Family Blessing*. In it I met a man who long before me had discovered the "blessing" of blessing his children. Inspired by Rolf Garborg's suggestions and testimony, I began preparing new blessings to use during these sacred moments with my daughters. With each new blessing, a biblical vision for my daughters was enlarged along with my vocabulary for expressing to God my heart's desire for them.

Many bedtimes have come and gone since I first opened the pages of this book. The two little girls have become women, and the bedtime routine we once knew is now a precious memory. Along the way there have been poignant moments of blessing that even now, as I call them to mind, bring a lump to my throat and tears to my eyes. Moments in dorm rooms and airports where we embraced and prayed one last prayer and one last blessing before the miles separated us. Moments at graduations, baptisms, and other significant events when I would look into the eyes of my grown-up "little girls." With my hands on their shoulders and familiar words of blessing on their heads, my heart overflowed again and again with familiar longings that the Father of infinite blessings would satisfy them beyond all that their earthly father could hope for.

Today I can look into the eyes of two more little girls, and what I see is not only the eyes of their mother; I see the eyes of the next generation. The longing in this grandpa's heart is the same as was the longing in the heart of this father when he first read the pages of *The Family Blessing*; the longing that one generation would commend the works of God to another (Psalm 145:4 NIV) and declare the praiseworthy deeds of the Lord (Psalm 78:4 NIV).

The Family Blessing is about more than another nice family tradition to practice. It is about the great *"I AM"* declaring His glory from one age to the next. May the Lord grant each reader's heart to overflow with blessing on the heads of their sons, daughters, and grandchildren. And may this new edition bring great joy to the coming generations through Jesus Christ and through the blessing of their parent's hands.

David Michael
PASTOR FOR PARENTING AND FAMILY DISCIPLESHIP
BETHLEHEM BAPTIST CHURCH — MINNEAPOLIS, MINNESOTA
PRESIDENT, CHILDREN DESIRING GOD
www.childrendesiringgod.org

TO MARY,

my precious wife for over forty-five years,

my most ardent friend, encourager,

counselor, and companion,

and the mother of my two most

cherished gifts from God,

Carlton and Lisa.

In 1989, when I wrote the first edition of *The Family Blessing*, my son, Carlton, was a twenty-year-old college student and my daughter, Lisa, was a seventeen-year-old senior in high school. Today I have five grandchildren, the oldest of which is now seventeen and a senior in high school. It is truly amazing how quickly life passes by. As I think about this, I am reminded again of how important it is that we make the most of each day we have with our families—especially how we need to treasure them and bless them while we have that privilege.

In these past twenty years I have had countless opportunities to share about blessing as a way of life, and I have been overwhelmed by the number of people who are longing to be blessed and desire to become people of blessing. It has been a joy to be able to speak God's favor and power into their lives—so many of them receiving these powerful words for the first time. In this new edition, I have included several of their stories. I know that you will be moved by them as I have been.

God is a God of lineage. Many of His promises to the people of Israel were about what He would do for their children if they obeyed. This goes to show that we are not an end unto ourselves. What God is doing in us doesn't begin or end with us. It began long generations before we came along; and when we allow God to work in our lives, it has a direct effect for good upon our children and generations to come, as illustrated in Exodus 34:6–7. What a legacy of blessing!

Many people influenced my life as I grew up—pastors, teachers, family, friends—but none more than my mother, father, and maternal grandmother. By her life, my grandmother showed me how to give thanks in everything. My mother was the fifth one of fourteen children, and she inherited my grandmother's heart. She taught me how to love unconditionally and how to forgive. Dad was the youngest of ten and had seen the devotion and commitment of his parents to each other and to God, watching as they read God's Word and prayed for their children. My fondest childhood memories of my dad involve waking up and finding him on the couch in the living room with his Bible open on his chest, his eyes closed and his hands folded in prayer for his three boys and others. Their stories and others' throughout this book show how blessing can become a legacy for generations to treasure.

Though intended as a gift for new parents as an encouragement for them to start the practice of blessing from day one, this edition of *The Family Blessing* can be used by all ages and for all relationships.

As you begin to read *The Family Blessing*, I ask that you do so with a prayer that God will make His truth known to you and that you will be encouraged to put the practice of blessing to work in your own life. I am more certain of the value and power of blessing than ever before and have seen God's hand at work in the lives of both the blessing-receiver and the blessing-giver.

May God bless you with fresh insights into His love and care for you, and may you become a person of blessing as you read this book.

Rolf Garborg
I would love to hear about your personal experience with blessing. You are invited to visit my Web site: www.rolfgarborg.com

The Lord bless you, and keep you;

The Lord make His face shine on you,

And be gracious to you;

The Lord lift up His countenance on you,

And give you peace.

NUMBERS 6:24-26 NASB

BLESSING BEGINNINGS

I still remember the scene: It was a balmy January evening in San Juan, Puerto Rico, in 1972. The nighttime street noises came freely through the open louvered window of the bedroom as my young son, Carlton, lay sound asleep.

I don't remember how long I simply stood by his bed that night, thinking about what a treasure he was. So many times before Carlton was born I had watched fathers with their young children. Now that I had a son who was nearly three years old, I wanted so desperately to be a good father to him.

Lord Jesus....

Take this blessing

of mine and use it

for Your glory.

Carlton didn't stir when I sat on the edge of his bed. As I leaned over his little body, I thought, *Lord Jesus, You showed us how much You care for these little ones when You took them in Your arms and blessed them. Now I want to do the same for my child. Take this blessing of mine and use it for Your glory.* Then I placed my hand gently on his head and whispered into his ear a blessing I had heard so many times in church, adding to it his name:

The Lord bless you, Carlton, and keep you.
The Lord make His face shine upon you and
be gracious unto you;
The Lord lift up His countenance upon you
and give you peace.
In the name of the Father, and of the Son,
and of the Holy Spirit. Amen.

It seemed so natural—so right. I felt as if I had obeyed God by doing this.

Before I rose to leave Carlton's room, I kissed him on the cheek, told him I loved him, and wiped the remaining tears from my face. Then I lingered there in the darkness and breathed a prayer of thanks to God for giving us this gift of a son and for blessing him. Little did I realize that the scene would be repeated thousands of times in the years to come.

That was the first night I gave my son a blessing. The idea was new to me, and I didn't fully understand what it was about. But after talking with another Christian father who gave his children a blessing every night, I had become convinced that this simple practice could transform our children's lives.

That year a recently released best-seller caught my eye: *The Christian Family* by Larry Christenson. In it the author, who at the time was the pastor of a church in San Pedro, California, clearly and biblically showed us God's order for the family and how we can practice the presence of Jesus in the home. I was immediately taken by the simplicity of the message in this book and began to recommend it to others.

This simple practice could transform our children's lives.

When an opportunity came to invite Larry to Puerto Rico, I gladly took advantage of it. He agreed to come and spend a week at our mission, teaching and sharing with us. One evening I asked Larry about a section in his book that dealt with the Christensons' practice of speaking a blessing on their children individually as they put them to bed each night. He said that he and his wife, Nordis, had been living in West Germany with their four young children when they first heard of the idea. It was a custom that was practiced by a couple they had met, Hans-Jochen Arp and his wife, Elisabeth.

Hans-Jochen told them how he would speak a blessing on each of his six children as they went to bed. Even if they were already asleep when he came home late, he would go into their bedrooms and bless them.

Larry and Nordis were so impressed with the idea that they went home that very night to bless their own children. First, they explained to them what they were doing and why. With four children, it took awhile to give everyone an individual blessing. But they did and continued to do it faithfully until each child was grown. Now Larry was sharing the idea with others.

The idea made sense. After all, we knew that many pastors bless their congregations at the end of each Sunday church service. Often they hold out their hands toward the people in a symbolic gesture of covering and then recite a benediction from the words of Scripture, such as the one the high priest Aaron spoke over the ancient Israelites:

The Lord bless you, and keep you;
The Lord make His face shine on you,
And be gracious to you;
The Lord lift up His countenance on you,
And give you peace.

NUMBERS 6:24-26 NASB

Then they may add words, such as: "In the name of the Father, and of the Son, and of the Holy Spirit. Amen."

Just as the pastor of a congregation has an opportunity to bless, we realized that parents as priests in their households have a similar privilege. They can speak at home the kind of blessing pastors speak to their churches.

As we talked with Larry on into the night, I became convinced that this family practice was right for us as well. What I didn't realize back then was how many benefits could come from making this commitment to bless my children.

So I made a decision. Whenever and however possible, I would bless my child every day. And I would begin that night.

After I'd given Carlton a blessing that evening, Mary and I agreed together to commit to this practice every night as we tucked him into bed. I could hardly wait for the next night to come so I could do it again, this time with Carlton awake.

During our discussion, I had already begun thinking of how it would be to have two kids to bless each night. As we continued talking, the realization came to me: We weren't done with the blessing this evening. I already *had* two children. Mary was just three months away from giving birth to our second child. Why not start now to bless them both? So I reached out my hand, placed it on Mary's stomach, and said, "Lord, I don't have any idea who it is You have for us in here, but I commit this gift of a child to You." Then, speaking to that unborn baby with my hand still on Mary, I spoke the blessing, just as I had with Carlton.

On April 23, 1972, Lisa Faith Garborg entered this world "sunny-side up," and she hasn't quit smiling yet. No doubt one

What I didn't realize back then was how many benefits could come from making this commitment to bless my children.

reason for her joy is that she has been blessed every day by her fathers—both earthly and heavenly—since even before she was born.

Carlton and Lisa are now adults with children of their own and both of them are continuing this practice with their own children. They also still receive blessings from us as the opportunity presents itself and welcome them as they did as young children. Their desire to continue to receive these blessings and to give them to their own children is just one indication of the impact it has made on their lives. We all know that this practice of blessing is not just a bedtime ritual.

Let's look at the significance of the blessing from a biblical standpoint to discover why it can become such a meaningful part of daily family life.

Blessed shall you be in the city,

and blessed shall you be in the country.

Blessed shall be the offspring of your body and the

produce of your ground and the offspring of your beasts,

the increase of your herd and the young of your flock.

Blessed shall be your basket and your kneading bowl.

Blessed shall you be when you come in,

and blessed shall you be when you go out.

DEUTERONOMY 28:3–6 NASB

CHAPTER TWO

THE BIBLICAL BLESSING

When God launched Abraham onto a course that would fulfill his destiny, He sent him from his parents' home into unknown territory. No doubt Abraham's excitement over his future was mixed with considerable apprehension over what lay ahead—the same kind of apprehension most of us felt when we first launched out on our own, leaving our parents' home forever.

How did God choose to prepare Abraham for the days ahead and to encourage him along the way? He provided a *blessing*:

I will make you into a great nation and I will bless you;
I will make your name great, and you will be a blessing.
I will bless those who bless you,
and whoever curses you I will curse;
and all peoples on earth will be blessed through you.

GENESIS 12:2-3 NIV

With these words the Lord spoke to Abraham a blessing of greatness, promised further blessing in the future, and said He would make the man a blessing to others—even a channel of blessing to the entire world. No doubt in the years to come, whenever Abraham faced challenges, these words from God strengthened and sustained him.

Throughout the Bible we find ample evidence that the God of Abraham was a God of blessing. In fact, the words *bless* or *blessing* appear in Scripture in some form or another about seven hundred times. Apparently Abraham, along with countless other people in the Bible, needed and welcomed the grace, power, and encouragement that could be poured into their lives through God's blessing.

But what is a blessing? The word has a variety of meanings in modern English, so let's look at two ancient biblical words to define what is meant by the term.

Throughout the Bible we find ample evidence that the God of Abraham was a God of blessing.

The Old Testament Hebrew word for blessing is *berakah*. To the ancient Hebrews, a *berakah* was the transmittal or endowment of the power of God's goodness and favor, usually through the spoken word and often with the accompanying act of the laying on of hands.[1] For Abraham, the *berakah* was God's spoken declaration of favor that would convey God's power to make him into a great nation and able to transmit that divine favor and power to the whole world.

The Hebrews believed that the spoken word carried great power for good or evil. Most ancient peoples were convinced, as the Hebrews were, that words once spoken take a life of their own. So when a word of blessing was given, the speaker could not retract it.

That was the case with Isaac's blessing, which was given mistakenly to his younger son, Jacob, rather than to his firstborn, Esau (Gen. 27:1–40). In this Bible story, we read that Jacob tricked his blind father into thinking he was Esau, so Isaac placed his hands on Jacob and pronounced on him the blessing of the firstborn child that rightfully belonged to Esau. Once Isaac spoke the words, there was nothing he could do to take back the blessing, even though it had been gained by deceit. The most this saddened father could do was to speak another blessing on Esau.

When a word of blessing was given, the speaker could not retract it.

Benedictions (spoken blessings) such as Isaac's were commonly spoken by fathers to their children. They were also given by people in authority to those under their authority, as in priests to a congregation. Such benedictions always included the name of God.

In the New Testament, the word most often translated as "bless" is the Greek verb *eulogeo*, from which we get the words *eulogy* and *eulogize*. It means literally "to speak well of " or "to express praise."[2]

As in the Old Testament, this blessing was often the act of calling down God's gracious power on someone. One clear example of this act in the New Testament is when Jesus blessed the disciples just before He ascended to heaven by promising that God would send the gracious power of the Holy Spirit on them (Luke 24:48–51).

FOUR TYPES OF BLESSING

One way to better understand blessings for our present purposes is to make a distinction according to the giver and receiver of the blessing. Using this criteria, there are four types of blessing found in Scripture:

1. A blessing *spoken by God to people*

This was a benediction by God, promising His favor, such as the blessing given to Abraham.

2. A blessing *spoken by people to God*

When we "speak well of" or "express praise" to God, then we're blessing Him, as David did: "*Bless* the Lord, O my soul, and forget none of His benefits" (Ps. 103:2 NASB). The apostle Paul echoed that sentiment when he wrote to the Ephesians, "*Blessed* be the God and Father of our Lord

Jesus Christ, who has *blessed* us with every spiritual *blessing*" (Eph. 1:3 NKJV).

3. A blessing *spoken by God or people over things*

Deuteronomy 28 is filled with this kind of blessing. God promises to pour out His favor on the material resources of the Israelites if they obey Him: "*Blessed* shall be...the produce of your ground and the offspring of your beasts.... *Blessed* shall be your basket and your kneading bowl" (Deut. 28:4–5 NASB).

People also spoke blessings over things as a way of dedicating them to God and setting them apart for His favor. The most common example is the blessing of food, an ancient Jewish custom that continues in the Christian community. Jesus showed the great potential power of such a practice when He blessed the loaves and fishes, calling down God's miraculous power to multiply them (Matt. 14:19–21).

4. A blessing *spoken by one person to another*

This was done in the name of God, who is the source of all blessing. Isaac's blessing of Jacob is one example of this kind; Aaron's blessing on the Israelites is another.

In this last category, please note that the word *blessing* can have both a general and a specific meaning. The general meaning can be referred to by the literal translation of *eulogeo*: "to speak well of, to express praise."

This is the sense probably intended when Jesus told His

disciples, *"Bless* those who curse you, pray for those who mistreat you" (Luke 6:28 NIV). Thus, Paul was obeying the Lord's command when he replied to his persecutors with gracious speech: "When we are cursed, we bless...when we are slandered, we answer kindly" (1 Cor. 4:12–13 NIV).

The more specific meaning of blessing is the intentional act of speaking God's favor and power into someone's life, often accompanied by a gesture such as laying hands on the person. This is the kind of blessing spoken by Isaac to his son Jacob, and in turn by Jacob to his sons (Gen. 48:8–49:28). It's the type of blessing Jesus gave to His disciples (Luke 24:50) and to the children (Mark 10:16).

In *The Family Blessing* we will look at both the specific and the general meanings of blessing within the context of family life. When the power of the spoken word for good or evil in our daily conversations at home is recognized, we can learn to use that power intentionally to bring blessing to our children.

How blessed is everyone who fears the Lord,

Who walks in His ways.

When you shall eat of the fruit of your hands,

You will be happy and it will be well with you.

Your wife shall be like a fruitful vine,

Within your house,

Your children like olive plants around your table.

Behold, for thus shall the man be blessed

Who fears the Lord.

The Lord bless you,

And may you see prosperity all the days of your life.

Indeed, may you see your children's children!

Peace be upon God's people!

PSALM 128 ADAPTED FROM NASB

CHAPTER THREE

BLESSING THE FAMILY

The hit musical play and film *Fiddler on the Roof* has tugged at the heartstrings of thousands of parents with its charming story of love and conflict in family life. Many parents can identify with the hopes and fears, the convictions and questions of Jewish Papa Tevye and Mama Golde as they struggle to rear their children in a godly way and to help prepare them for happy and productive adult lives.

One of the most poignant scenes from the play shows the family at the table of the Sabbath meal. When all have gathered, they perform the ancient customs associated with that meal. The mother lights the Sabbath candles, prays, and then joins her husband in singing to the children the "Sabbath Prayer," a simple song of blessing that expresses their desires:

May the Lord protect and defend you,
May He always shield you from shame;
May you come to be in Yisroel [Israel] a shining name.

May you be like Ruth and like Esther,
May you be deserving of praise;
Strengthen them, oh Lord,
and keep them from the stranger's ways.
May God bless you and grant you long lives,
May the Lord fulfill our Sabbath prayer for you.
May God make you good mothers and wives.
May He send you husbands who will care for you.
May the Lord protect and defend you,
May the Lord preserve you from pain;
Favor them, oh Lord, with happiness and peace,
Oh hear our Sabbath prayer. Amen.[1]

I launched both my daughters out of the nest with a special gift.... a personalized CD for each of them with 31 blessings....

~ David Michael

What Christian parent doesn't hear echoed in those words the deepest sentiments of his or her own heart? And yet how many of us have a regular setting where such powerful words can be expressed to our children?

Christian families can adopt the Jewish community's ancient tradition of parents giving their children a benediction simply by personalizing this biblical custom according to their family's needs.

You may say or sing a blessing; you may express it daily, weekly, or on special occasions. You can select a Scripture to use or create your own blessing based on Scripture. However you choose to bless your children, the family blessing—acted out so beautifully on the stage in this play—can become a real life scene in your own home. And it will confirm your children in godliness by speaking into their lives the grace of their heavenly Father.

On January 2, 1998, our daughter Lisa married Jason Rovenstine. Lisa committed her life to Christ at a young age and always wanted to live for Him. As she grew in her faith and into a young woman, I don't think there was anything more important to Mary and me than she find a man who would love and cherish her and be faithful to her on every level. Jason was clearly that man.

... I [also] challenged my future son-in-law to pick up the mantle of responsibility for blessing not only my daughter but my future grandchildren and great-grandchildren!

~ David Michael

I think we fell in love with him before she did as we watched him court her and honor her in his conversation and actions. At their wedding, the officiating pastor pointed to a vase atop the organ and said, "I want to direct your attention to the white roses. There are twenty-five of them—one for each year of Lisa's life. Jason's heart-felt love and appreciation is now expressed to Lisa in keeping herself for him these twenty-five years. God bless you." With tears in her eyes, Lisa thanked Jason and kissed him. I don't know what you would have done then, but I wept! The presence of Christ was so evident and some guests commented afterward that they recommitted themselves to Christ and to following Him in purity.

Before the wedding, Jason and Lisa had prepared little coil-bound flip books with several blank pages in each. Placing one on each of the tables at the reception, they encouraged their guests to write their thoughts on those pages. Some were funny, some gave advice, some were memories of friendship, but all were from the hearts of their friends. I wanted to write one for them, too, but that evening was not the time. I waited another day and then, finally, early in the morning on the following Sunday, I wrote this note:

Lisa and Jason, it is now Sunday morning, January 4, 1998, and I couldn't sleep. I am overwhelmed by God's goodness. I am also profoundly lonesome. Lisa, I will miss you...your hugs, laugh, smile, face, piano playing, spirit, and joy of life. I will miss you sitting on my lap, even at age twenty-five! I am so proud of you!

Jason, I don't know what a father is more prayerful about than who his daughter marries. I rejoice at God's "over and above what I could ask or think" answer to those years of prayers. I bless you with Lisa. Love her! Cherish her! Hold her! Forgive her! Make her laugh! Honor her! Encourage her! Care for her! Help her! And bless her every day of your lives together! And, lest I forget, be fruitful with her! I would love some more grandchildren! Love, Dad

P.S. TLBYAKY, TLMHFSUYABGUY. TLLUHCUYAGYP! ITNOTF, TS, ATHS!

The P.S. above is the first letter of each word from the Numbers 6:24–26 blessing. I often use that, or at least the first seven letters, *TLBYAKY*, in my notes and e-mails to my family when space or time was limited. Several years ago, Mary presented me with a special gift. It was a personalized license plate for my car that read *TLBYAKY*. That has provided me with countless opportunities to bless total strangers. I love it.

OUR CHILDREN'S HIGHEST GOOD

When Jesus came to earth two thousand years ago, He came to accomplish one overwhelming task: to give Himself to our highest good, that we would know and love God with all our heart. Just read what He prayed to His Father in John 17:3–4: "And this is eternal life: that men can know you, the only true God, and that men can know Jesus Christ, the One you sent. I finished the work you gave me to do. I brought you glory on earth."

Again in Luke 10:25–28, when Jesus was questioned by a teacher of the law on how to gain eternal life, He replied with a question: "What is written in the law?" The teacher answered, "Love the Lord your God. Love him with all your heart, all your soul, all your strength, and all your mind. And you must love your neighbor as you love yourself." Then Jesus said to him, "Your answer is right. Do this and you will have life forever."

The single most important concern we should have as parents should be the same primary concern Jesus has for us: *We must make it our ultimate goal to help our children know and love God with all their hearts.*

How do we do that? One of the simplest and most powerful ways to help children know and love God is to give them a daily, concrete encounter with His power and favor by laying hands on them and speaking a blessing over them.

The concept of a parent speaking a blessing on a child may seem strange, but it is scriptural. It's an ancient and respected custom dating back to biblical times. In fact, the family setting for the blessing apparently predates its use in the public setting; the priest or other official who spoke benedictions on the people of Israel was

> *We must make it our ultimate goal to help our children know and love God with all their hearts.*

only supplementing the most basic of blessings—the one given by the father to the children.

Even those who have never given or received this kind of blessing have probably caught glimpses of it in various contexts, such as benedictions in church services or the scene just described in *Fiddler on the Roof*. Several Old Testament stories focus on this custom, some of which were previously mentioned: Isaac's blessing of Jacob (Gen. 27); Jacob's blessing of his sons and grandsons (Gen. 48:8–49:33); the priest Melchizedek's blessing of Abram (Gen. 14:18–20); the high priest Aaron's blessing of the Israelites (Num. 6:23–27); and the prophet Balaam's blessing of the Israelites (Num. 23:7–24:9).

HOW WE USE THE BLESSING IN OUR HOME

In our family, the approach we used in blessing our children was quite simple.

Each evening at bedtime, I would lay my hands on the head of each of my children and speak the blessing that appears in Numbers 6:24–26, adding at the end the words "in the name of the Father, and of the Son, and of the Holy Spirit," and personalizing it to each child by including his or her name.

It was that simple. We just spoke the same blessing to our children each night. And they came to depend on it as a token of security and a sign of their parents' continuing love for them.

Of course, even though our blessing was simple, busy schedules seemed to conspire to complicate matters. A little flexibility helped us maintain the blessing in our household over the years.

Thank you for opening my eyes to the fact that we have been authorized to bless.

~ Heather H.

In biblical times, certain people were considered to be endowed with a special authority to bless or to curse: priests, prophets, and fathers, for example. But a blessing could be given by anyone. This is especially important to know in establishing the blessing in your home today.

The primary role of blessing in our household has always rested on me as the husband and father. But because of work-related travel, I've not always been present to give the blessing.

Knowing that anyone can give this blessing relieved some of my concern about my travel schedule. When I was away from home, Mary assumed the responsibility of blessing the kids and often blessed them with me when I was home. In single-parent homes or homes where the children are raised by relatives or guardians, it should be the spiritual head of the household who gives the blessing, whether that is a mother, father, grandparent, or caretaker.

When I was away on business, I would call home as often as possible. After catching up on the day's events with both children, I would bless them individually over the phone.

Frequently, if the kids thought I was going to forget or if they had to leave, they would say, "Dad, can I have my blessing now?" They wouldn't miss it for any reason, and their commitment to the practice helped assure that the family blessing was a permanent fixture in our home.

JESUS BLESSED THE CHILDREN

When Jesus walked here on Earth, He was subject to the same laws of physical nature as we are. He experienced hunger, thirst, and the need to rest.

He also was subject to many of the same laws of human nature as we are. Perhaps that's why He had to be alone from time to time. As a human, He must also have tired of having the disciples around day and night for three years. He not only heard their arguing and bickering about who was going to sit where in heaven (Mark 10:35–41), but He also knew their thoughts

Often Jesus encouraged adults to learn from children.

(Luke 9:46–48). Knowing what was in their hearts must have caused Him some pain.

Nevertheless, there was one group of people I'm certain Jesus would have welcomed any time: the children. Often He encouraged adults to learn from children, saying we need to be like them to enter the kingdom of God (Matt. 18:1–6). And on one very special occasion, He allowed us to know the depths of His concern for the little ones:

> *Some people brought their small children to Jesus so he could touch them. But his followers told the people to stop bringing their children to him. When Jesus saw this, he was displeased. He said to them, "Let the little children come to me. Don't stop them. The kingdom of God belongs to people who are like these little children. I tell you the truth. You must accept the kingdom of God as a little child accepts things, or you will never enter it." Then Jesus took the children in his arms. He put his hands on them and blessed them.*
>
> MARK 10:13-16

Blessing our children is as vital in today's world as it was in Jesus' time.

Taking these children in His arms, placing His hands on them, and blessing them was not at all an unfamiliar behavior to Jesus or to those around Him. He was simply doing what a good Jewish father or rabbi would have done. His action was a lesson to His listeners then and to us today about the significance of children and the need to actively communicate God as Father to them.

At times I've thought, *Oh, to have been one of those children that Jesus held in His arms and blessed.* But, in all likelihood, those little children were not aware of the significance of that experience. Though Jesus is the Son of God and His blessing was certainly precious, the greatest value of His one-time blessing of those children may well have been that it taught the adults who watched how they should treat their children. For those who followed His example, the most important blessings their children would receive were those they received from their families thereafter.

Blessing our children is as vital in today's world as it was in Jesus' time. With temptations in our society pulling at them from all directions, children need a wall of protection surrounding them. And the earlier we begin strengthening that wall, the safer they'll be when the temptations come.

The wall they need is provided by our love. It can be reinforced, brick by brick, each time we bless them.

May the Lord answer you when you are in distress;

may the name of the God of Jacob protect you.

May he send you help...and grant you support....

May he give you the desire of your heart

and make all your plans succeed....

May the Lord grant all your requests.

PSALM 20:1–2, 4–5 NIV

CHAPTER FOUR

MAKING IT WORK

It's been determined that the blessing is an ancient biblical practice that countless parents through the ages have maintained as valuable and even indispensable. Nevertheless, at this point I can anticipate the question: "But does it *work*?"

If "work" means some mechanical connection between the blessing and certain immediate, specific behaviors of children, that would be difficult to prove. Any connection of that nature would amount to little more than manipulation.

However, a useful measure of the positive impact of practicing the blessing can be found in children's attitudes toward the blessings in homes where it is practiced. In our home, an occasional situation has provided a telling anecdote that illustrated just how much Carlton and Lisa valued the blessing.

THE SECURITY OF THE BLESSING

During one particular time in my life, when work required international travel lasting from two to five weeks, I called home to bless the children about once a week. On the eve of one of those trips, I was tucking eleven-year-old Lisa into bed when she asked, "Dad, how long will you be gone on this trip?"

"Oh," I said, "about four or five weeks."

"No," she persisted. "How many nights will you be gone — exactly?" I went to count on my calendar the exact number of nights and then returned to her room.

"Thirty-two nights," I said. "Why?"

"Well," Lisa mused, "then you have to give me thirty-two blessings. Now."

I chuckled as I considered her request, but I thought, *Why not?* So I agreed. Anticipating that this would take awhile, I lay down beside her as I placed my hand on her head. Then I began: "The Lord bless you and keep you, Lisa.... " I went on to say the full blessing from Numbers 6:24–26 that I had spoken over her for years.

When I was done, Lisa said, "That's one, Dad. You've got thirty-one more to go!"

Some time later, when I finished the last one (with Lisa counting all the way), she chirped, "Okay, Dad. Now you can go on your trip." The job was done. Lisa felt secure. She knew that everything would be fine even though Dad was a long way from home. Of course, the fact that I spoke the blessing to her thirty-two times was no more powerful than speaking it once to her in faith.

However, my blessing for every night represented to her the security of my commitment to her welfare.

CHILDREN DO LISTEN

As you consider how children's positive attitudes toward the family blessing indicate its significance in their lives, you might wonder whether the particular words spoken really mean anything to the children themselves, especially if they're young. You might conclude that all the kids are actually responding to is the fact that they're receiving a few undivided moments of parental attention.

I agree that one critical factor in the blessing's ability to convey God's love to kids is the parental attention which they desperately need. However, many children also listen carefully to what's being said.

One friend of mine has been blessing his children every night for several years now. He began one night with a simple "God bless you with grace and peace in Jesus' name. Amen." But over the following few months, as he considered all the kinds of blessings he wanted his children to experience, the list grew. Now each night he lays his hands on his children and imparts:

God bless you with grace and peace,
power and protection,

health and healing,
holiness and godliness,
abundance and prosperity,
and all the fruit and gifts of the Holy Spirit,
in Jesus' name. Amen.

That's a formidable list of blessings to remember, even for an adult, and it's only because they are repeated each night that he's able to call them to mind.

Nevertheless, one evening my friend was exhausted from a particularly demanding day, and as he blessed his children, he accidentally forgot a portion of the blessings. Immediately his young daughter interrupted.

"Dad," she insisted, "don't forget the power and protection. That's important."

Even a six-year-old was paying close attention, knowing that every word was important.

Kids can be like Chinese bamboo trees.

THE CHINESE BAMBOO TREE

In our high-tech world, we're becoming more and more conditioned to expect the instantaneous. But I'm a little skeptical of techniques that promise instant changes in our children. No doubt the results of blessing our children, or anyone else, are *sometimes* visible immediately. But usually results of these blessings come much later. And sometimes only God is the witness.

Zig Ziglar tells the story of the Chinese bamboo tree. When the seed is planted, instead of sending up a shoot, it goes dormant. No amount of nurture and attention can rouse it from its sleep. The Chinese bamboo lies dormant for five years with no apparent signs of growth. Then in one year it suddenly grows over sixty feet into a mature tree.

Even though the tree reveals no visible signs of growth for several years, it still requires the care that would be given to any other seed. Without such care during its incubation, it would never become a tree. Since the farmers know this, they continue to care for the seed—despite the lack of any visible results.[1] Kids can be like Chinese bamboo trees. As parents we may do everything we know is right but then despair if we don't witness any immediate growth or change of heart. Sometimes we even become so anxious over their progress that we "dig them up" with our frustration and undo the good we've done.

This situation may be especially frustrating when a child has once made a commitment to the Lord. Often when the teenage years arrive, those sweet, obedient children may begin to question and rebel against both their parents and their faith. They may even appear to be going full speed in the wrong direction, doing things they know are wrong.

How should a parent respond if that happens? Should you force them to accept your faith "or else..."? Or do you keep on "hoeing" around them, tending to the things you know will produce a mature tree someday?

Though it's easy to give up at such a time, we must keep in mind that we really want our kids to have their *own* faith in God, not their *parents'* faith. Sometimes the transfer of faith is swift and smooth; sometimes it's slow and painful. But if we stay the course, prayerfully doing what we know is right, sooner or later the tree will grow—and when it does, it will be strong and well-rooted.

Your commitment to continue blessing your children during these difficult months or years shows them an element of your faith they might never see otherwise. Your steady, unwavering demonstration of confidence in what they'll become will help them mature in accordance with those positive expectations.

THE BENEFITS OF BLESSING

I want to affirm that God desires to lavish Himself on us and reward our obedience to Him openly and abundantly— and, at times, quickly. His reward comes to us in many ways, as His promises indicate:

He will meet all our needs (Phil. 4:19).

He will give us the desires of our hearts (Ps. 37:4).
He will send angels to guard us (Ps. 91:11).
He will withhold no good thing (Ps. 84:11.).

One of the benefits of blessing our children is an element of openness and honesty, both toward us and toward God. This has been illustrated through the years by the candor they've shown in confessing things they've done that they knew were wrong.

I remember one particular night, when Carlton was about eleven years old and he called us to his room. We had already tucked him in for the night, prayed with him, and given him his "hands-on" blessing. But alone in the dark, he had been thinking about something he had done that day. He knew that what he had done was wrong, and God would not, as the blessing said, "give him peace" until he confessed and made things right.

God desires to lavish Himself on us and reward our obedience to Him.

It didn't take long for the confession to come and the tears to flow. We listened as he prayed and asked God to forgive him and help him not to do that again. We talked with him and assured him that God had heard his prayer and forgiven him. We verbally forgave him also. Then we prayed again with him.

As we were walking to the door, he said, "Mom and Dad, I feel like a big bag of junk just left me!" Mary and I rejoiced with him in his release from guilt, and we knew that God was at work in him. We have marveled again and again at how both of our children have remained open with us about what's going on in their lives.

Earlier we noted that our greatest responsibility to God as Christian parents is to raise children to know and love Him with all their hearts. At the same time, our greatest responsibility to our children is to exhibit the heart of God to them. What they see in us has great bearing on what they understand God to be like.

Our greatest responsibility to our children is to exhibit the heart of God to them.

When we have something we dearly treasure, we take special care of it, making certain that it's not damaged or destroyed. We accord it a place of honor and would never consider taking out our frustration or anger on such a treasure. Instead, we protect it in every way possible.

The same is true of our children. After years of reinforcing their sense of security, acceptance, and self-esteem through blessing, the last thing we want to do is destroy what we've worked so diligently to cultivate. So the blessing of our children becomes a daily reminder that we have built a relationship with them and an attitude within them that must be protected—even when we have reason to be angry.

When my son was young, I bought a new car that was by far the nicest car I had ever owned and was certainly the most expensive. I loved that car and took special care of it, washing it frequently and maintaining it faithfully.

One spring morning, however, I noticed a footprint on the hood. Upon closer inspection, I also saw a dent in the hood where the footprint was.

There was little question that it was Carlton's footprint. My heart sank and my anger rose. I'm now grateful that he had already left for school! As I stood by the front of the car, I wondered why he would have climbed on the hood. Then I spotted my golf clubs on the shelf above the front of the car, remembered the warm spring weather, and understood what had happened.

As I drove to work, I noticed that the dent in the hood was right in my line of vision; every time I sat behind the wheel of that car, I would see it. Because it was in such a prominent place, my immediate thought was to get it fixed. After all, isn't that what insurance is for?

Nevertheless, in my heart I heard the Lord saying, *Just leave it. It's not that bad,*

When we have something we dearly treasure, we take special care of it.

and besides, the car's not yours anyway. It's Mine. Everything you have is Mine. And so is your family.

I thought of the close relationship I'd built with my son and how much I treasured him. Then I thought of how close I'd come to allowing something else I treasured—something of infinitely less value—to hurt that relationship. I had blessed my son for years; was I going to "curse" him with hurtful words now?

No. Instead, I felt God telling me, *Why not use that dent as a positive reminder that your son needs your prayers?* After all, the Lord had given me this boy so I could care for him, pray for him, and show him the heart of his heavenly Father.

Years later that old car expired. It had clocked 128,000 miles by the time it died and nearly as many prayers of gratitude for God's goodness in giving me my son.

I did question Carlton about the dent. He had no idea of what he'd done. He'd simply acted impulsively on his desire to swing the golf clubs. So he apologized, asked me to forgive him, and agreed to use the stepladder next time. Needless to say, our relationship was stronger than ever before.

Does the blessing of your children work? Is it worth the time and commitment? The answer to both is clear: Yes! Absolutely!

Our experience and that of many other families show that the blessing works. Of course, just how it works is more difficult to explain. We can observe the sense of security and concern that is obviously produced by speaking words of encouragement to a child day after day, and we can recognize that such encouragement is bound to impact the child's life for good. But blessing him or her seems to convey much more.

As the ancient Hebrews recognized, words of blessing spoken in the name of God are able to transmit the power and favor of God.

Those who have faithfully spoken it year after year would probably all agree on one point: Blessing others is practiced *because it is the right thing to do.* Based on the examples given in Scripture, God rewards those who bless as well as those who are being blessed.

God rewards those who bless as well as those who are being blessed.

FEEDBACK FROM THE BLESSING-RECEIVERS

Up to now, this book has illustrated the significant difference a regular blessing can make in the lives of children. But perhaps children can provide the most convincing testimonies of what the blessing can mean to them. Following are recent letters written to me by my children, Carlton and Lisa. Their words reflect the importance of receiving the blessing now that they are both grown with children of their own.

Dear Dad,

I can remember receiving a blessing from you every day as I grew up, being a scared little kid who needed comfort and reassuring; but the blessing brought peace to my heart. This is something I wanted to do for my own child. It is pure simplicity. I knew how much it meant to me to know that my parents loved me enough to ask God to bless me every day, and I really feel like He did.

I have been blessing my daughter, Christina, every day since she was born. It has become a ritual in our house, as it was for me when I was a kid. As she grew older she asked for it and reminded me when I'd forget—like I reminded you.

Our own little blessing dynamic evolved over time, and we went to "two-a-days." In addition to bedtime, I started blessing Christina every morning on the way to school after we prayed for the day. She began blessing me, too. There were many days that I thought it meant more for me to hear those words from her than for her to hear them from me.

She was about ten years old when I asked her to write down what she thought about getting blessings every day. She thought about it and wrote, "It makes me feel so good. It helps me sleep and feel safe. It makes me happy and have happy thoughts, not

> *In a powerful sense Dad's whole life was a blessing.*

nightmares—I sleep like a log. When I get a blessing in the morning, it gives me courage and makes me feel strong when I start the day. It brightens my day. I feel good when I bless my dad because I feel like it helps him through the day and it helps to take away pain." She couldn't be more right.

Now, by the time this book is published, I will be forty years old and Christina, my little girl, will be almost eighteen and graduating from high school! I have watched her go from braces to driver's ed. to ACT tests and—GULP—her upcoming graduation and journey into the world as she leaves for college. What a treasure it is to watch your little lady blossom into a young woman. I have continued to bless her over the years and will never stop. In fact, I think I bless "extra hard" now that she has so many big decisions in front of her. She has blessed me as well, not only with words, but with her tender spirit and unconditional love.

I've also realized another important aspect of blessing, which is the impact of our words on our kids and on others. Hearing those warm, loving words every day builds a strong self-image and high self-esteem. So many people hear angry and hurtful words, many times from their own parents. How much better it is to fill the hearts of our children with words of love!

I think love is the core value that fuels all relationships, including our own relationship with God. It is what makes blessing so powerful. God's blessing is a promise to us that He loves us and will watch out for all His children. He will never give us more than we can bear even though it may not always seem like it in these troubled times. He loves us unconditionally. Passing that blessing on to our children and instilling that sense of comfort, value, and worth into their lives is so important.

To all the parents who read this—you don't have to be perfect, but what's wrong with trying, right? Since we have been entrusted with such precious cargo, I want to encourage you to listen to your children, tell them you love them, protect them, defend them, discipline and instruct them, praise their uniqueness, inspire them to be their best, and lead by example. Our children are a gift God has given us to care for and return to Him one day. So, with all the love in your heart, bless them.

Dad, thank you for listening, forgiving, understanding, and not judging, and for your constant encouragement, words of blessing, and, more than anything, for loving me for who I am.

— Carlton

Dear Dad,

Thank you for making the commitment to bless us every night and sticking to it all those years. The blessing was such a special gift that you gave to us; it was free, yet so valuable! I never tired of receiving the blessing or the big bear hug that went along with it. I always felt so affirmed, secure, accepted, and loved. It took only a minute to speak those familiar words from Numbers 6, but those sixty seconds were powerful! It was a bonding time that I looked forward to each night, and it often turned into a time of reconciliation that brought peaceful closure to the day as it was impossible to give or receive a blessing with anger or unforgiveness in our hearts. Because you gave us the blessing nightly, it never let bad feelings build up. It forced us to work out our differences just as the Bible instructs us to not let the sun go down upon our wrath. That consistency brought security. You never withheld your blessing as punishment for our bad behavior because the blessing was not a reward to be earned: It was a gift.

The beauty of the blessing is that we team up with God. We speak the words and God empowers them and imparts His favor through us as we step out in obedience and faith. So often as you spoke the blessing I sensed the Lord's presence. He would bring life and authority to your words as you spoke them, and I knew His love for me in a very intimate way. I am convinced that it is because of the blessing that it was so easy for me to know Jesus personally. The blessing also taught me to receive God's gifts and not strive to earn them, since my role in the blessing was all about receiving. Lastly, I believe it helped to shape my image of God. I always pictured Jesus with a smile on His face and His arms outstretched, beckoning me to come to Him. I know this stems from the love and joy you, as my earthly father, expressed to me as you blessed me. This made it easy to view my heavenly Father in the same way.

Dad, you did your part in faithfully pronouncing the blessing, but God also did His part in accomplishing every aspect of the blessing in my life. He truly has blessed me and kept me faithful to Him, shown me His face and His grace, and given me His peace. Thank you, Dad, for leaving this legacy for us to follow.

My husband and I have counted it a privilege to continue this legacy with our own kids, Sofie, Elle, Vienna, and Von. They look forward to it just as I did when I was a kid, and I have a feeling this tradition will continue for many more generations. We look forward to seeing the fruit of it in their lives, as I have certainly seen in my own life.

—Lisa

May God himself, the God of peace,

sanctify you through and through.

May your whole spirit, soul and body be kept

blameless at the coming of our Lord Jesus Christ.

The one who calls you is faithful and he will do it....

The grace of our Lord Jesus Christ be with you.

1 THESSALONIANS 5:23–24, 28 NIV

CHAPTER FIVE
GETTING STARTED

The most difficult part of any job for me is getting started.

Sometimes the tasks I delay are as simple as replacing a lightbulb. I can rationalize, excuse, and defend this behavior with comments like, "We can see just fine without that light," or "Do you realize how much it costs to burn that thing?" or best of all, "What good will it do? It's just going to burn out again anyway!"

Finally, when I complete the job, I find not only that the bulb took all of two minutes to replace, but also that it really is nice to have the extra light. Getting started with the blessing of your children is a little like replacing a lightbulb. It really isn't much work when you actually do it; it doesn't take much time, and the results are better than you thought.

However, I can't give you a simple formula that says, "Do these five things and all your troubles will end." You see, there's no right or wrong way to bless your children. A blessing of any sort is still a blessing—something good and powerful and precious. The only mistake you can make is to decide that for fear of doing something wrong, you'll do nothing at all.

Let's explore some of the common questions in getting started.

> *A blessing*
> *of any sort*
> *is still*
> *a blessing —*
> *something good*
> *and powerful*
> *and precious.*

1. *What age should my children be when I start and stop the family blessing?*

The answer is simple. At what age do you want them to begin receiving the benefits of being blessed, and how long do you want that to continue?

It's not important whether they're fifteen years or fifteen months, or whether or not they understand the words you are speaking. The longer you wait to begin, the fewer opportunities you will have to impart God's grace to them through the family blessing.

Take full advantage of the time you have—start today. The overwhelming majority of all we will ever learn in life, we learn before we start school. Of course, all is not lost if that time in our children's lives is past. God can and will impart His blessings. But nothing can be gained by further delay.

By the same token, children are never too old to be blessed. They need the favor and power of God throughout their lives. So why would we ever stop the family blessing?

Older kids I know who have been blessed since an early age don't consider it a childish ritual they've outgrown. On the contrary, they now cherish the blessing more than ever. So even if children move far away, they can be blessed daily, long distance, in our private prayer times.

2. *Is bedtime the only time of day to bless my children?*

Absolutely not. God is up and awake all the time and is always ready to bless. Since it's God who actually does the blessing, any time is the right time.

However, structure and consistency are important, especially to young children. So think through your day and find the best time for your family. It may be bedtime or mealtime. It may even be when your children leave for school so they can launch out on the new day with a blessing still ringing in their ears.

If the best time for your family isn't immediately obvious, experiment a bit. Tell your kids what you want to do and why. If they're older, ask for their suggestions.

Take full advantage of the time you have — start today.

3. *Should the blessing be spoken daily?*

Again, there are no rules; however,

a daily blessing obviously gives you more opportunities to bless your kids. Many families prefer to have a regular time of family blessing on a weekly basis.

4. *How do I know what to say?*

Take a look at the blessings in between each chapter. One of these might meet your needs. Or try using a concordance to find all the occurrences of the word bless in the Bible; among them you'll find a number of blessings, and you'll also learn a great deal about how blessings were given in biblical times. Of course, there is always the option of creating your own blessing based on Scripture. When we agree with God's Word, we know we are in agreement with His will.

5. *Does the blessing have to be the same every time?*

Not at all. You can vary the blessing however you see fit. As I mentioned earlier, structure and consistency are important, especially for younger children. There is a certain value to repeating the same words over and over every night during a child's growing-up years; it provides them a sense of stability, of predictability, of security. You don't need to seek novelty for its own sake. But if you think a fresh form of the blessing would benefit your children, why not try a different one? You may even want to learn a whole series of blessings based on Scripture and rotate them regularly. In fact, the blessing doesn't have to have a set form at all. Like prayer, it can be spontaneous.

6. *Who should provide the blessing in the family?*

As Christians we're all called to bless and be a blessing. In our family, as the husband and father, I assumed the primary responsibility of blessing our children, but Mary often joined me. She also spoke the blessing to the kids in my absence. Some families prefer to have both parents give the blessing together. In single-parent homes, it should be the spiritual head of the household, whether that is a mother or a father. Even our children have given the blessing to each other.

7. *Does blessing your children replace prayer?*

Definitely not. There are three vital kinds of conversation with God that we share with our children. These conversations are like strands woven together to form a single braid, which collectively are infinitely stronger than individually. On this braid, I believe, hang all the other disciplines we desire to develop in our children's Christian lives. And though the three are similar, they serve very distinct purposes:

Strand One: Prayer *for* our children — interceding for them as the family's priest, lifting them and their needs up to the throne of God.

There are three vital kinds of conversation with God that we share with our children: praying for them, praying with them, and blessing them.

Strand Two: Prayer *with* our children—introducing them to God, bringing them into our own conversations with God, modeling for them a healthy pattern of regular communication with the Father.

Strand Three: *Blessing* our children—to complement and strengthen the other two, reflecting the goodness, power, and fatherly heart of the God we talk to when we pray for and with our children.

GUIDELINES TO CONSIDER

When you begin the practice of blessing your children, here are a few guidelines:

1. *Before you begin, explain to children old enough to understand what you're planning to do and why you believe it's important.*

Children will be much more cooperative and appreciative if they understand why you want to bless them and why it's important. Provide answers to their questions as well as you can.

A dear friend of mine was visiting with me one evening. As we began talking about our kids, I told him about our practice and of the benefits of blessing our children. He liked the idea and decided to begin blessing his three children, who were ten, eight, and four at the time.

Nearly a year later I saw him again, and he could hardly wait to tell me the news. "Guess what? I've been blessing my children ever since we were together last time. It's great! I went home, took each one in my arms individually, put my hand on the child's head, and gave the blessing from Numbers 6."

He was grinning widely as he told his story. "You know," he observed, "each of the children responds differently when I bless them. One gets right into it. He snuggles up to me when I hold him and almost purrs in the process. The second one just receives it nonchalantly, as a normal part of what Dad does. But the little guy stands at attention. His arms are at his sides, and he's stiff as a soldier. To him, this is God touching him, and he wants to be as good as he can."

The kids each had a different understanding of what the blessing was about. But the important point is that from the beginning, each one had some understanding of what was going on, and it held meaning for him or her.

2. *Hold your children in your arms when you bless them.*

Gary Smalley and John Trent have an excellent chapter in their book, *The Blessing,* called "The First Element of the Blessing: Meaningful Touch." In it they chronicle the value of parents touching their children, citing examples and teaching from a spiritual, psychological, and physical perspective.[1]

Hugging has always been as much a part of my extended family as saying "hello" or "good-bye." We virtually never do one without the other. Whichever family member is involved makes no difference. Whenever we greet or leave one another, we hug.

In fact, I hug almost anybody. When I hug folks who aren't family members, I often hear them comment, "Oh, I really needed that!"

One of my son's buddies, a hard-working, no-nonsense, superjock type, came to our house some time ago, and I gave him a hug. When I let him go, he said, "I like coming to the Garborgs' house. They give hugs here." Now he also gives me hugs on Sundays after church.

From reading the Bible, we can conclude that the patriarchs knew the value of human touch. Jesus knew the value of it as well. He took the little children in His arms and held them when He blessed them. We should, too. It's a way of telling children that we accept them as they are, and it opens the door for them to receive the blessing when we give it to them.

From reading the Bible, we can conclude that the patriarchs knew the value of human touch.

At the same time, it's important to note that some people feel uncomfortable hugging others. Perhaps their families were not especially affectionate physically, or certain experiences in their lives have caused them to resist close contact of the sort I am describing here. That's okay. A hand on the shoulder or on the arm can be a meaningful substitute. I

would, however, encourage you to explore appropria[...]
in which you can experience the closeness that can only c[...]
through a more physical expression of affection.

3. *Place your hand or hands on the heads of your children when you bless them.*

This action is also modeled to us by Jesus. And no wonder — the gesture has great spiritual significance and symbolism connected with it.

The Bible teaches that the "laying on of hands" was used for consecrating people for service to God, imparting the Holy Spirit, and praying for the sick to be healed. In the church today, it's also used in the symbolic gestures of baptism, confirmation, and ordination.

Larry Lenning, in his book *Blessing in Mosque and Mission*, notes that in the biblical context:

> The act of laying on of hands was a sacred act through which the blessings of God were given. The hands of the blesser were not sacred. But through these human instruments, God bestowed His benediction, power, grace and mercy.... In the light of the Jewish background of the New Testament and the early Church and with the evidence of the New Testament itself, the laying on of hands was a sacred act through which God bestowed varied blessings.[2]

The symbolism of "covering" our children is important here. We depict to them through this gesture the protection and care with which God shields them.

4. *Always include in your blessing an invocation of the name of God.*

It's the name of the one true God that separates this blessing from all other blessings in the religions of the world. Many non-Christian cultures have forms of blessing similar in intent and wording to those of the Christian faith. What sets the Christian blessing apart as a divinely powerful experience is the invoking of the name of the true God. When we contemplate the sheer awesomeness of God and the infiniteness of His power, we can begin to understand what can happen at the mere mention of His name. And we can identify with David's feelings when he cried out to God in Psalm 103:1: "Bless the Lord, O my soul, and all that is within me, bless his holy *name*" (NASB).

The form of God's name you use is, of course, up to you, according to what is most meaningful to your family. Many Christians use the church's tradition of invoking God with the name of the Holy Trinity: "In the name of the Father, and of the Son, and of the Holy Spirit." Others prefer simply "in Jesus' name." In either case, the powerful name of our Lord sets apart our blessing as a vessel of *His* grace.

5. *Teach your children to speak blessings on themselves on days when you forget or are unable to give the blessing for some reason. Help them understand that the blessing of God still rests on them and protects them.*

Younger children especially look forward to the comfort and security of the blessing, and they may become unsettled if it's not given, for whatever reason. It is important to avoid encouraging kids to think that God's blessing, and especially His protection, comes only through the spoken words of a parent. If we emphasize to young ones that the family blessing is simply one of many ways the Lord pours out His favor and power and that they have the privilege of speaking a blessing as well, then we can allow them to feel secure in God's love and in our own.

Here's a brief review of the main points we've made in this chapter to help you get started:

- Start today, no matter the age of your children.
- Bedtime is a good time to bless your kids, but by no means is it the only time. Explore what works best for your family, with regard to the time of day and frequency of the blessing.
- Choose words for your blessing by referring to the suggestions in this book or finding them in Scripture. The words don't necessarily have to be the same every time, though there are benefits to continuity.

- Blessing should never take the place of prayer. Blessing, prayer *for* your children, and prayer *with* your children are all important ways of including children in our conversations with God.

- Explain to your children what you're doing and why.

- Hold your children in your arms when you bless them, and place your hand or hands on their heads.

- Always invoke the name of God in your blessing.

- Teach your children that the family blessing is only one of the ways God uses to bless and protect us.

- Above all, begin today!

The God of love and peace will be with you....

May the grace of the Lord Jesus Christ, and the love of God,

and the fellowship of the Holy Spirit be with you all.

2 CORINTHIANS 13:11, 14 NIV

CHAPTER SIX

A POSITIVE COVERING

So far we've focused on blessing in a specific sense: the kind of blessing we read about in the Bible in which one person intentionally and explicitly invokes the goodness of God into the life of another person through the spoken word. Now we'll explore the blessing in a more general sense: how the power of words operates in our daily lives to strengthen or to hurt those around us—not just within family relationships but within all relationships.

We know God is a God of blessing; the Bible makes that clear. But the Bible also shows that God's people are to be a *people of blessing*. In Matthew 5:44, Jesus commanded us not only to bless our loved ones but to bless our enemies, as well. The Lord pours out His power and favor on us, and, like Abraham, He appoints us to be a blessing. He has delegated to us the role of conveying His grace to others, and one of the primary means by which we can do this is through the power of our daily words.

"Death and life," says the book of Proverbs, "are in the

power of the tongue" (Prov. 18:21 NASB). Nowhere is this reality clearer than in the dynamics of family life. The words that parents speak to their children day in and day out, even in casual conversation, create an atmosphere in the home over time that either choke and poison their young spirits or nourish and strengthen them. The results can be devastating or life-giving: "Reckless words pierce like a sword, but the tongue of the wise brings healing" (Prov. 12:18 NIV).

He has delegated to us the role of conveying His grace to others, and one of the primary means by which we can do this is through the power of our daily words.

We have a daily choice as parents to speak life or death to our children. Speaking "death"—destroying their self-esteem with negative labels, nicknames, household reputations, or self-fulfilling prophecies—is what the Bible calls "cursing"; we will deal with that issue specifically in chapter eight. But even if we rarely inflict these kinds of verbal injuries on our children, we may still be guilty of draining the life from their spirits by our negligence or reluctance to "speak well" of them.

After one television interview that I had on the subject of blessing, the producer told me that her father had a nickname for each of his children. He would introduce them as "This is the fat one; this is the one that never does anything right; this is the dumb one; this is the ugly one; and this is the one that will never amount to anything." I was amazed. She was now in her midthirties and still carrying that load of "trash talk" around. How very sad, and how very unnecessary.

Recently while traveling in Kiev, Ukraine, with my dear friends Mark and Vicki, I was stunned to hear their comments after I spoke at a dinner to a group of about twenty booksellers. I shared some thoughts on blessing and cursing as taught in my book. At the end of the evening, Mark, who is a leader in the Christian publishing industry, said, "You have no idea how appropriate your comments were tonight. Throughout my whole childhood, my mother's nickname for me was 'Stoop'—short for 'stupid.' " I was dumbfounded. And then Vicki, who has written over forty books, looked at me and told me another extraordinary story. "I haven't spoken to my father in two years," she said, "but the last thing he said to me was 'You are such a disappointment.' " My heart sank to my feet.

I could hardly believe what I had heard. My first thought was to hug them both and bless them on the spot, but others at the dinner interrupted my conversation, and before I knew it the opportunity had passed. Later, I went to bed with a heavy heart for my friends. I woke up at 3:00 a.m. and couldn't shake the heaviness I had been feeling for them. As I listened to a favorite worship album over and over, I wept and prayed for Mark and Vicki. Finally I drifted back to sleep, but not before deciding that I would share my thoughts with them and ask for their permission to bless them, even if others were present.

At 8:00 that morning a small group of us met in a tiny room for breakfast. After chatting for a few minutes and eating a bit of food, I started to tell them what I had been thinking about during the night. I could barely talk as all the emotions of the night before welled up in me again. I told them that if they would let me, I would like to pray and ask God to break the effects of those curses they had carried throughout their lives, and to bless them. They readily agreed, and I rose and stood behind them as I prayed.

I don't know how long I prayed for each, but I knew that God was at work. As I placed my hands on Mark's head, we both shook with sobs as I blessed him with the Aaronic blessing from Numbers 6:24–26. God was breaking the hold that this "curse" had held on him for nearly fifty years.

Then it was Vicki's turn. Again God moved in her heart to let her know that God, her heavenly Father, was not "disappointed" in her. And we wept again.

When we met again a few weeks later, Mark told me that he had shared this experience a few times with others since he'd returned from Ukraine, and that each time he would weep again as he realized what happened and the release he felt from this curse.

This can happen to anyone who has labored under the weight of a lifetime of curses and negative input. The expression "garbage in, garbage out" usually means that what we feed on (put in) determines our behavior (what comes out). But, in this situation, it means that all the "garbage" that others have dumped on us throughout our lives can be thrown out for good when we fill that space with blessing. We are sometimes led to believe that we are who we are and we can't do anything about it. We can't do it ourselves, but we can call on God to permanently dispose of all the garbage from our past into the pit that is covered by His Son's blood. May God let it be so in you today.

SPEAKING EULOGIES

Think about the English word for "speaking well" of someone that comes from the Greek root *eulogeo*: *eulogy*. When do people present eulogies? At the person's funeral! It's sad that we wait until people are gone before we eulogize them, before we "speak of them well."

Proverbs 25:11 says, "A word fitly spoken is like apples of gold in settings of silver" (NKJV). An appropriate expression of appreciation is an adornment

"A word fitly spoken is like apples of gold in settings of silver."

Proverbs 25:11 NKJV

placed on the recipient that brings honor to the person, whether alone or in the presence of others. Now is the best time to adorn our children with such blessings.

This general kind of blessing is not limited to words spoken *about* our children. It can also refer to the words we use when speaking *to* them. Words that show respect can elevate their self-esteem, their level of performance, and their attitude.

I've heard business managers give commands to their associates as though they were some sort of drill sergeant, rather than using a polite request. Whenever workers are told, "Do this" or "Bring me that," their morale and productivity suffer. If we would consider what a difference could be made by prefacing our requests with a genuine, "Would you mind," or "Could you please," we could create a more joyful, efficient workplace. Then, when the job is finished, a "Thank you" or "I appreciate what you did" could be an added blessing.

If kind words are appropriate in the workplace, they're even more appropriate at home.

If kind words are appropriate in the workplace, they're even more appropriate at home. Family blessings often take on the form of a kind word prefacing a request. Look at what Paul essentially says in Ephesians 4:29: "When you talk, do not say harmful things. But say what people need—words that will help others become stronger. Then what you say will help those who listen to you." These kind words can be said in private or public. They will always be appreciated and could often result in changed behavior on the part of the recipient. First Peter 3:8–9 illustrates the very nature of blessing:

> *Finally, all of you should live together in peace. Try to understand each other. Love each other as brothers. Be kind and humble. Do not do wrong to a person to pay him back for doing wrong to you. Or do not insult someone to pay him back for insulting you. But ask God to bless that person. Do this, because you yourselves were called to receive a blessing.*

Of course, the reason we bless our children or anyone else by speaking well of them is not to control them or to squeeze a little more from them. We bless people because it's the right thing to do! Period. Receiving a blessing in return is simply a bonus that God provides for obeying Him.

GENUINE WORDS

In order for a blessing of this type (the kind word or expression of praise) to be well-received, it must meet at least two conditions. First, it must be *warranted*. You may have to think hard to find a quality you can praise in someone— even, at times, your own child. Keep looking; you'll find it.

An unwarranted blessing is empty and hollow. It's not really a blessing at all.

For a blessing to be well received, it must be warranted and sincere.

The second condition is that it must be *sincere*. An insincere compliment is easily detected, and it leaves a bitter taste in the mouth of both the giver and the receiver. But a sincere compliment does more to build the confidence of those around us than almost anything else we can do.

During the early spring of our son's senior year in high school, Mary and I were talking with the parents of some of his classmates. His school was a small Christian institution with a graduating class of only eleven. (To this day Carlton likes to say he graduated in the top ten of his class.) Several of these kids had actually been together since they'd started school a dozen years earlier.

We were reflecting on how the parents of those kids had bonded, as well. We had all watched them grow. Four of the boys had played sports together since the seventh grade. We had witnessed the character development that comes from teamwork and competition as well as seen their development as friends and as Christians.

As we reminisced about the uniqueness of this class of eleven, a desire to do something special developed. We decided to have an "appreciation night." We did not realize at the time how powerful the evening would become and the impact it would have on everyone present.

Only the parents and their senior-class children were present. The conversation over dinner was light and relaxed. Following the meal, the program began. There were plenty of laughs as we "roasted" each senior. Then the room drew quiet.

One by one, each father came to the front and declared to his child those things that he most appreciated about him or her. Many tears were exchanged between father and son or father and daughter. One dad prefaced his words with a confession: "I have never really told you this before...."

Each father's list of comments was specific and individual, making them much more meaningful. Their "words fitly spoken" included treasures such as these:

"You are the type of daughter, the type of person, who has helped me grow."

"You have a heart for God."

"God will reward you for all the hidden sacrifices you have made."

"My only regret is that I didn't have ten more just like you!"

"I see the treasures God has put in you beginning to blossom."

"I see Jesus in you."

These fathers' heartfelt remarks were "eulogies" in the best sense of the word—expressions of praise given before it was too late. Their power to bless their children was intensified because these words were spoken by someone significant in their lives: their fathers.

At the end of each comment, father and child embraced. In conclusion, the blessing found in Numbers 6:24–26 was sung to a melody that one of the fathers had written.

That evening provided an opportunity for feelings of gratitude and encouragement to flow—in some cases, perhaps, feelings that hadn't been expressed in years.

If you haven't been regularly blessing your children with kind words that come from a heart of gratitude, start now. Begin speaking well of them and expressing praise to them today. Desire the best for your children by taking the initiative. Make an active commitment to bless your family daily, allowing God to do His part.

May the Father, from whom His whole family

in heaven and on earth derives its name,

out of His glorious riches strengthen you with power

through His Spirit in your inner being,

so that Christ may dwell in your hearts through faith,

that you, being rooted and established in love,

may have power, together with all the saints,

to grasp how wide and long and high and deep

is the love of Christ, and to know this love

that surpasses knowledge — that you may be filled

to the measure of all the fullness of God.

EPHESIANS 3:14-19 ADAPTED FROM THE NIV

CHAPTER SEVEN

A BLESSING IN A NAME

If the words we parents speak to our children have the power of life or death, then consider the phenomenal power resident in the one word we speak to them far more than any other—the word they will hear throughout their entire lives—the child's name.

In the biblical world, a person's name was inextricably bound up with the person's nature. The authority to give a name was seen in some sense as the authority to control the one named. Consequently, the giving of names was a serious affair. And it still is today, whether the name is a given name, a surname, a nickname, or a reputation.

Our name is undoubtedly one of our most treasured possessions. It is part of what distinguishes us from everyone else, and in many ways it shapes who we become, for good or

The first gift we parents give a child is his or her name, and it's a gift that will last an entire lifetime.

for ill. The first gift we parents give a child is his or her name, and it's a gift that will last an entire lifetime. Because of this significance, selecting a name for our children must be considered carefully. We can literally bless or curse our children with the name we give them.

We can further bless our children by making certain that they know what their name means.

The name that can most significantly serve as a vital form of constant blessing and encouragement to our children is their first or given name. Great thought and care should go into selecting these lifelong labels; something that's merely "cute" or popular at the time may not be the best choice. Most importantly, we should ask God to make clear His choice for our child's name.

Once we give them the name we believe is right, we can further bless our children by making certain that they know what their name means and why we chose it for them. Then every time we call them by name, we're blessing them.

HOW OUR CHILDREN WERE NAMED

When I first went to Puerto Rico in early 1966, our mission had several Christian leaders come as guests. During the two weeks they were with us, I was tremendously impressed with the Christlike spirit I saw lived out in one of those men in particular. His name was Carlton Spencer. When he and the others left, I told the Lord that if I ever had a son, I would name him Carlton because the deepest desire of my heart was that he, too, would be Christlike. Three years later, Mary and I got our son, and as I had told the Lord, we named him Carlton.

When our daughter came along three years later, we named her Lisa Faith. Lisa means "consecrated to God"; she has been consecrated to Him since before she was born. As for her second name, the meaning is clear. On various occasions when the subject of faith has come up, she has stated with delight, "My middle name is 'Faith.' "

Throughout both our children's lives we've reminded them of why we chose their particular names for them, at the same time letting them know our prayers and desires for them. In fact, since the time they were small, we've had hanging on our wall at home a plaque with each of our family members' names and their spiritual meanings.

GOD'S INTEREST IN OUR NAMES

We find examples in the Bible of just how important the naming of a child can be to God. Jesus, for example, was given His name by God before He was born. It was the name the Father had carefully chosen, because it signified that He would be the Savior (Luke 1:31; 2:21).

When Jesus' cousin, John the Baptist, was born, we're told that his parents surprised their family and friends with a name that broke the tradition of naming a child after a relative. John's father, Zechariah, gave the boy the name "John" in obedience to God's specific instructions, and as soon as he did, his voice returned—ending a nine-month discipline God had imposed on him for not believing that his wife could bear them a child (Luke 1:18–20, 59–64).

In the Bible we read of several people whose names changed, usually to signify some important change in their identity resulting from a life-changing encounter with God. Abram became Abraham (Gen. 17:5); Sarai became Sarah (Gen. 17:15); Jacob became Israel (Gen. 32:28); Solomon became Jedidiah (2 Sam. 12:24–25); Simon became Peter (Matt. 16:18); and Saul became Paul (Acts 13:9). In each case the new name was part of a blessing, a reception of God's power and favor into their lives.

Today some folks change their names as well, often for the same reason. One common way to change is to begin going by the middle name instead of the first name (or if the child is known by the middle name, to switch to the first). That happened with one of my friends who, at his conversion, changed from using his first name, Thomas, to using his middle name, Paul. He decided that instead of being the "doubter," he would become a man of faith.

For this reason, it's important to make sure that both given names have a special significance. You never know whether your child might someday choose to go by their other name.

THE BLESSING OF A SURNAME

Surnames, or "last names" as we call them in the United States, tell much more about our kids than just where they sit in the classroom. Surnames declare our heritage. They carry with them the reputations of those who went before us — whether it was our grandfather who was known for bravery in the war or our older brother who was known for harassing his schoolteachers. Surnames may also reveal our ancestors' occupation, our nationality, our race, or even our religion.

Though our last names can be a great blessing, some of us may wonder how. Consider my own name: Garborg. One day a friend of mine and his son saw me walking down the street, and the boy asked: "Who is that, Dad?"

"Rolf Garborg," his father replied.

"What?" said his son. "Why would anyone want to be called 'Rough Cardboard'?"

A LINK TO OUR HERITAGE

Despite the fun folks may have with some of our surnames, these titles form important links to our heritage. Knowing something about our ancestors can be a useful way of filling

Knowing something about our ancestors can fill our surname with special meaning, thus making the name a blessing.

our surname with special meaning for our children, thus making the name a blessing. Research into our family tree might even help us find ancestors whose character, behavior, or vocation can serve as role models for our children.

If we look back at our own family history, we may see continuity not only in occupation or trade but also in character. Scripture assures us that "the sins of the fathers" are visited "upon the third and fourth generations" (Exod. 20:5), and we might note from experience that the same is often true of the blessings, as well. Some studies of family trees reveal a remarkable string of criminals spanning many generations. Others have shown a similar line of statesmen, clergy, or educators.

Of course, we should emphasize to our children that we can choose which of these character examples in our past we will perpetuate. If necessary, we can even pray to break any curses that may have hung over our family for years. It's up to us whether our descendants will be able to point with legitimate pride to our example and claim a godly heritage for themselves embodied in the blessing of an honored surname.

THE MEANING OF A SURNAME

If you do some research into the literal meaning of your surname—or even into its historical associations—you may discover some special significance in it that will make it a further blessing for your children. The spiritual significance of a surname like "Christian" or "Bishop" is obvious. But even with an unusual name like my own, hidden meanings can be surprising.

My two brothers and I have long been involved in the distribution of Christian literature throughout continents and regions such as Central and South America, the Caribbean, Europe, Africa, Asia, the South Pacific, and Canada. Between the three of us, we have literally covered the globe with Christian literature.

On one of my brother Kent's trips to Hong Kong, he noticed a file with the name "Garborg" on it. Next to it were two Chinese characters. He found out from a Chinese clerk that those were the two characters for the name "Garborg" written in Chinese. He asked if those marks were just a transliteration of the sounds of our name, or if they had actual meaning.

"Oh, they have actual meaning," said the clerk. "This one is how we write 'gar,' and it means 'to spread,' while this one is 'borg,' which means 'abroad' or 'over a wide area.' "

Was it simple coincidence that when all of us were

working abroad in the distribution of Christian literature we discovered the meaning of our name in Chinese to be "to spread abroad"—or can there be more significance to our surnames than we realize? In either case, it was a great blessing to these three brothers to realize that every time someone called us "Garborg," he was naming the vocation God had given us.

THE BLESSING OF A GOOD REPUTATION

> *A good reputation is one of the greatest blessings our children can carry.*

Another meaning of the word "name" is *reputation*. "A good name," the Bible says, "is more desirable than great riches; to be esteemed is better than silver or gold" (Prov. 22:1 NIV). A good reputation is one of the greatest blessings our children can carry.

Earning a "good name" begins during childhood. Teachers not only observe the work that our children do but also the character qualities they exhibit, such as a positive attitude, proper response to authority, setting and reaching goals, school spirit, neatness, and getting along with others. Whenever Carlton and Lisa brought home their report cards, the first place I looked was on the back of the card where these observations about character appeared. They were infinitely more important to me than my children's grades. And when we had parent-teacher meetings, the discussion focused not on their grades but on their behavior.

The blessing of a good reputation for our children is obvious. It goes before them and opens doors of opportunity for them. It becomes their servant, and if they treat that servant well and don't abuse it, it will stay with them their whole lives.

Timothy, the apostle Paul's trusted companion, had that type of reputation. When Paul learned of the need in the Philippian church, he wrote:

> *I hope in the Lord Jesus to send Timothy to you soon. I will be happy to learn how you are. I have no other person like Timothy. He truly cares for you. Other people are interested only in their own lives. They are not interested in the work of Jesus Christ. You know the kind of person Timothy is. You know that he has served with me in telling the Good News, as a son serves his father (Phil. 2:19–22).*

What parent wouldn't want to have their son or daughter carry the lifelong blessing of that kind of reputation?

We're all responsible and accountable for our own reputations. But we can also influence others in the reputation they earn. As parents we have the greatest opportunity and obligation to do just that. We should be sobered to realize that if we don't choose to be a positive influence on our children in the development of their "name" in this regard, we will by default be a negative influence.

A "HOUSEHOLD REPUTATION"

Even within the four walls of one's home, a child can develop a reputation that serves to bless or curse. Most families probably recognize what we might call a "household reputation" among family members that labels a child in one way or another: "Well, Jill's just lazy"; "You know Gary—he never gives up"; "George will eat whatever doesn't eat him first."

When my family and I moved back to Minneapolis from Puerto Rico, the transition was an emotionally disruptive time for us all. Everything was turned upside down, especially for our kids—and worst of all for Lisa, who was just three at the time. She missed her playmates and the surroundings in which she was familiar, and she began to change from an energetic, buoyant, happy little girl into a whining, fussy, demanding one.

I wasn't dealing with her changes very well and soon found myself giving her negative reinforcement that only made matters worse. She was getting on my nerves, and even though I continued to bless her at night, I was counteracting those blessings with the negative responses I was giving her at other times of the day.

About that time my brother Kent gave me a book called *See You at the Top* by Zig Ziglar. One story that Zig told was especially appropriate to our struggle with Lisa's emotional change. He told of how his second daughter, Cindy, changed from being a whiner to being a happy child through the power of a positive reputation at home.

Cindy (at the time the middle child) had been saddled with expectations that she would be different in a negative way from her older and younger siblings. She responded to the expectations accordingly. Her father often said, "Why does Cindy whine so much? Why isn't she happier and more cheerful?"

When the Ziglars realized they were building a poor reputation in the family for Cindy, they began making an intentional change in the way they referred to her. Instead of "cursing" her with the reputation of a whiner, they began calling her "the little girl everybody loves because she is so happy."

The result? Cindy became a different child. She even changed her own nickname from "Tadpole" to "Happy Tadpole."[1]

> *Reaffirm those good qualities you know your child has.*

After reading that story, I began to practice this same approach on Lisa, reaffirming those qualities we knew she had. Whenever I saw her, I said, "How is my happy little girl who smiles all the time?" Amazingly, within a matter of days, the fussing and whining ceased and the broad smile appeared on her face again. She had been blessed by the new reputation she was given and began to live up to it. And she still does to this day.

THE BLESSING OF A NICKNAME

Somewhat related to a person's reputation is a person's nickname. If you doubt that even a nickname can be a blessing or a curse, simply ask yourself which would you prefer to follow you throughout your life and beyond: "Alexander the Great" or "Ivan the Terrible"?

Most nicknames are verbal caricatures which take a dominant feature, trait, action, or skill and blow it out of proportion. The problem with most of them is not so much that they're distorted, but rather that they exclude all other attributes or characteristics. No doubt Thomas had many strong points, but he is known as "the doubter." In the same way, Alexander was likely not "great" in every way.

At their worst, nicknames are intended either to intimidate or to put down; the cruelest of all are tied to race, physical appearance, or handicap. No wonder the literary critic

William Hazlitt once said, "A nickname is the heaviest stone that the devil can throw at a man."

Other nicknames, however, are based on positive character qualities: "Champ," "Sparkle," "Cutie." They can be a source of encouragement and affirmation, especially when parents use them to bless their children. Still other nicknames are meant as "pet" names or terms of endearment: "Sugar Bear," "Cookie," "Sunshine." These, too, can be a blessing as they signal to children their parent's affection and the special place they hold in the parent's heart.

Look for positive, praiseworthy qualities that you want to cultivate in your kids.

Even Jesus gave nicknames to some of His disciples. To wavering, impulsive Simon, for example, He gave the nickname "Rock" (Peter) as a way of affirming His confidence that Simon would indeed become firm in his character and his faith. No doubt that label made Peter want to live up to his name.

If you choose to use nicknames with your children, or with anyone else, for that matter, look for the positive, praiseworthy qualities that you want to cultivate in them. Give them names that will bless your children when you speak them, names that show value and approval, names that build up instead of tear down.

SPEAKING BLESSING THROUGH YOUR FAMILY'S NAME

Ultimately, of course, the particulars of one's name are much less important than the fact that they're written in God's book of life (Rev. 21:15). Nevertheless, the names our children bear—whether their given names, surnames, nicknames, or reputations—can be for them a source of great blessing. Since words have such an impact on who our children become and names have perhaps the greatest impact of all, we can bring God's grace into their lives by speaking over them names of blessing and by helping them discover a blessing in the meaning of the names they have been given.

May the God of peace,

who through the blood of the eternal covenant

brought back from the dead our Lord Jesus,

that great Shepherd of the sheep,

equip you with everything good for doing his will,

and may he work in us what is pleasing to him,

through Jesus Christ, to whom be glory

for ever and ever. Amen.

HEBREWS 13:20–21 NIV

CHAPTER EIGHT

BLESSINGS THAT HEAL

Webster defines a curse as "a calling on God or the gods to send evil or injury down on some person or thing; to damn." In this sense, the blessing is the opposite of the curse, which calls down God's grace on a person or thing. So we shouldn't be surprised that just as our day-to-day speech to our children can bless them with encouragement, it can have the power to curse them, as well. Even though most of us would never deliberately curse our children or friends, it can happen in many subtle ways, both by default and through ignorance of the effects of our behavior.

WHAT THE BIBLE SAYS ABOUT CURSES

We find a broad range of meanings for the more than one hundred uses of the words for "curse" in Scripture, but all the biblical curses had one thing in common: they contributed toward the destruction of the person or object being cursed. One particular biblical word for "curse" is the Greek word

> *"Reckless words pierce like a sword, but the tongue of the wise brings healing."*
>
> *Proverbs 12:18 NIV*

kakologeo. It is the opposite of *eulogeo*, the word for "bless" we looked at before that means literally to "speak well of; to express praise." Thus *kakologeo* means "to speak ill of; to revile." Just as positive words have the power to convey God's grace, negative words have the power to destroy.

The *kakologeo* type of curse has a real power to produce negative, destructive, even damning effects just as the blessing has a real power to produce positive, constructive, liberating effects. When we realize the harm done through this type of curse, we can see the need to replace it with words of blessing.

At the same time we might be sobered to realize that the curse injures not only the one who receives it—it hurts the one who speaks it, as well. Even mildly negative words, when they become a pattern, work their way down into our spirits to do damage in accordance with the biblical principle that whatever we sow, we'll also reap (Gal. 6:7–8).

Considering the grave consequences of the curse, we do well to search our own patterns of speech with our children to identify and root out the negative words that might be found there. We can start with a look at the negative label.

NICKNAMES AND REPUTATIONS

The nickname, as I've mentioned before, is a label that can bless or curse our kids. Though our intentions may be to show affection, we must be careful. Through our "terms of endearment," we may be saddling them with a less-than-complimentary self-image or an unfair focus on one negative characteristic.

In the previous chapter we mentioned the notion of a "household reputation," and it should be obvious how such a reputation can curse a child if it's negative. This kind of curse may take the form of negative *expectations* of a child. Negative expectations usually develop when our child has "failed" at something or has just not "measured up." We may tend to assume that the failure is somehow permanent or typical.

Such expectations may often be expressed in self-fulfilling prophecies like "You'll never amount to anything in life!" Sometimes they take the form of a rhetorical question like "Can't you do anything right?" Or we may even leave children on their own to fill in the blanks about our estimation of them: "Just who do you think you *are*, young man?"

COMPARISONS

When I was in grade school, one of my teachers tried to motivate me with this type of negative comparison. She would say repeatedly, "Now, Rolf, you can do better than that. Remember how well your older brother did when he was in this class!"

We usually mean well by these types of comments, but they are seldom received that way by the children. Typically, the recipients are always on the "short end" of the comparison and feel like failures when they hear them. They lose heart and tend to try even less to be as good as the one to whom they've been compared. This feeling becomes a curse that can stay with a person throughout an entire lifetime unless it's broken.

Often when people who've received these types of "curses" as children grow up, they become underachievers. Little wonder. They've been convinced since they were young that they weren't as good as the next kid.

As a child I felt this way to a great degree because what my teacher intended as a motivation, I received as an insurmountable obstacle and I gave up trying. My report cards often carried the disgraceful words, "Rolf does not work up to his ability." And I remember thinking, *What do they know about my ability?*

I knew I was loved and approved at home, but the "baggage" of mediocrity, this "curse" that I received in school, overshadowed the reinforcement I got at home. Even though I was reared in a warm Christian environment and went to church three times a week, it wasn't until I had a personal, public encounter with Jesus Christ as my Redeemer at the age of fifteen that this curse began to be broken.

When I knew for a fact that I was accepted by God, I began to accept myself as His creation—a creation He had said was "very good" (Gen. 1:31). Not mediocre! So I began to see those areas of strength I had, the gifts that God could use, and I stopped comparing my gifts to those of others.

I even began to hear things differently. Remarks I had previously received as put-downs now sounded more like compliments. God even brought new friends into my life, friends who would build on the new foundation He had laid. I was still the same gangly, clumsy, immature kid I had been earlier, but these new friends saw my potential and began to draw it out of me. In particular, Nelson Clair, the youth pastor in our new church, believed in me and showed it by spending time with me and challenging me to be all I could be in Jesus. I'll be forever grateful for the way his attitude of blessing helped to break the power of the curse I had accepted as a child.

When I knew for a fact that I was accepted by God, I began to accept myself as His creation.

NO MIXED MESSAGES

If we have made a conscious decision to speak a blessing on our children each day, then we also need to make a conscious effort to avoid cursing them. Otherwise we can inadvertently destroy much of the good God does through our blessing. We'll be sending mixed signals—and mixed signals are usually received for their *negative* value. As the apostle Paul asks, "Don't you know that a little yeast works through the whole batch of dough? Get rid of the old yeast that you may be a new batch" (1 Cor. 5:6–7 NIV).

I know what I'm talking about when I refer to these kinds of curses; sad to say, I've spoken them to my kids myself. And whenever I have, I've invariably felt rotten about it. I knew that I really didn't mean what I said—it just kind of "came out." But the damage was done.

This is one situation where the great benefit of regularly blessing our children has been clear. Whenever I spoke wrongly to my children, I couldn't put them to bed and bless them without first making things right.

THE BLESSING AS A BALM

In the ebb and flow of our busy lives today, we constantly encounter situations with our family members or fellow workers in which someone gets hurt. Emotional "cuts and scratches" are just part of daily life. They happen no matter how spiritual we are.

Ultimately, it isn't the fact that these abrasions occur which creates hard feelings and strained relationships. Rather, it's what we choose to do about them once they happen that makes them either a blessing or a curse.

With our kids, the potential for offenses is enormous. It might be as simple as not giving them the time they need or barking a "Can't you see I'm busy?" at them. Sometimes a slow response from our kids to do a task we've given them evokes an "If you know what's good for you, you'll be here in thirty seconds." These and other bumps and bruises build up during the course of a day, and unless they're dealt with when they happen, they'll be there when the kids go to bed. Worse yet, the children may be sent to bed as punishment.

Because our family had a fixed time for blessing our kids all those years, neither they nor we could go to bed angry. We just couldn't bless our children while we had a bad attitude toward them. We couldn't send them to bed without supper and then go in to bless them without making things right between us.

Can you imagine? You're angry with your son, so you send him to bed. Later, still angry, you go into his room, sit on the edge of his bed, give him a hug, put your hand on his head and say, "The Lord bless you and keep you (you disobedient little wretch), the Lord make His face shine

Speaking a blessing is like a soothing ointment, a healing balm that dispels the hostilities of the day.

upon you and be gracious unto you (even though what you really deserve is a swift kick in the britches), the Lord lift up His countenance upon you and give you peace (because you sure as shootin' won't get it from me). In the name of the Father, and of the Son, and of the Holy Spirit. Amen."

No way. Can't do it. Won't work. If you make a firm commitment to bless your children at bedtime, you'll find that it displaces the anger. It will be like a soothing ointment, a healing balm that dispels the hostilities of the day and allows both the offender and the offended to sleep in peace. I believe this is one way to obey the apostle Paul's command: "In your anger do not sin. Do not let the sun go down while you are still angry, and do not give the devil a foothold" (Eph. 4:26 NIV).

BREAKING THE POWER OF CURSES

Breaking the power of a family curse requires two steps: First, we must break any curses we're still under ourselves from our own childhood; and second, we must break the power of the negative words we may have spoken over our children.

Often the curses spoken over us years ago will reappear in

our home today as the "sins of the fathers" are "visited" upon subsequent generations. Just as physically abused children may grow up to become abusers themselves, children who were called "idiot," for example, are more likely to pass on that curse to their own children. If that's the case with us, we must take the attitude that with our generation, "the buck stops here."

FREEDOM FROM OUR OWN CURSES

If you're laboring under the weight of one of the kinds of curses I've described, the following insights may help. They aren't meant to be a formula as much as they are a pattern. Because God made us to be individuals with free wills, He works with each one of us in different ways. So perhaps these points, along with some good counsel from your pastor, can start you on the journey of breaking free from the curses of your past:

1. *Admit your need*. Denial only serves to cement the problem further and perpetuate its effects. Just as the Holy Spirit came to convict the world of sin, He also came to convict it of judgment (John 16:8). Curses are judgments other people have put on us, whether deliberately or unwittingly. Acknowledge that you've been judged, and the Holy Spirit can begin to free you.

2. *Identify as specifically as you can the nature of the curses spoken over you.* Do you labor under the feeling that you just can't measure up? Do you struggle with the image of yourself as an unintelligent person? Are you unable to get motivated in your career? Then search your heart and your memory for curses that may relate to those specific circumstances. If you can identify the specific curses, write them down.

3. *Recognize that through His death and resurrection, Christ has set us free from the power and effects of the curses of the enemy.* When the writer of Hebrews spoke of the need to "throw off everything that hinders" (Heb. 12:1 NIV), he included the hindrances of these curses we carry needlessly.

4. *Pray aloud by name for each curse to be broken.* For example, label each curse and pray through each one, "Father, in Jesus' name, I ask You now to break this curse over me. I renounce it — I will no longer submit to that judgment against me. In place of this curse, I receive now from You the blessing You have given me." After you pray to break each one, cross it out!

5. *Focus your attention on the blessing given us in Jesus — on what He has done for you, who you are in Him, and who you can become because of Him.* The power of sin and death is broken. The power of the curses we have carried is broken. We need only focus on Jesus and avail ourselves of His completed

work. After telling us to cast off hindrances, the writer of Hebrews goes on to say: "Let us fix our eyes on Jesus, the author and perfecter of our faith, who for the joy set before him endured the cross.... Consider him who endured such opposition from sinful men, so that you will not grow weary and lose heart" (Heb. 12:2–3 NIV).

6. *Forgive those who put the curses on you.* Forgiving those who have hurt us is one of the most difficult things we'll ever be called on to do. Nevertheless, it helps to remember the apostle Paul's words to the Colossians: "Forgive as the Lord forgave you" (Col. 3:13 NIV).

If we learn to forgive, trusting that God is in control, we can break the curse and walk in freedom.

The surest way to remain under the curse of another person is to refuse to forgive that person. If we learn to forgive, trusting that God is in control, we can break the curse and walk in freedom.

7. *Replace the curse with blessing, praise, and the Word of God.* The apostle Paul told the Romans: "Do not be overcome by evil, but overcome evil with good" (Rom. 12:21 NIV). You can overcome evil with good in at least three ways:

The first is by *blessing*. Once you've forgiven those who cursed you, bless them. Speak God's power and favor on them. The strongest "repellent" for a curse is a blessing.

The second way to overcome evil with good is by *praise*. When you praise God for who He is, what He's done, and who He has made you to be in Christ, you overcome the evil of the curse.

The third way to overcome evil with good is by the *Word of God*, which is "the sword of the Spirit" (Eph. 6:17). Memorize and repeat often the Scriptures that tell you who you are in Jesus.

BREAKING THE CURSES OVER OUR CHILDREN

Once we've begun to walk free of the curses spoken over us, we'll be free to break the curses over our children. The process is primarily the same—we must help our children through the same steps we've taken ourselves.

If the child is small, we'll have to pray to break the curses for them. We'll have to explain what Jesus has done for them in terms they can understand. And whatever age they are, we'll have to help them cultivate a pattern of blessing, praise, and memorizing Scripture to overcome the evil with good. With some curses such as nicknames, we can replace the curse with a blessing by giving the person a new name.

RECOGNIZING OUR PART

The most important part of breaking our children's curses, however, is to recognize those that we ourselves have spoken. As parents we must search our hearts and memories to discover what words we might have spoken that need to be renounced and replaced with words of blessing.

Perhaps the best place to begin is by asking our children themselves what words we've spoken that have injured them. Because the offender always has a shorter memory than the offended, we may be surprised at what they say. But it's critical to give our children genuine freedom to talk about this; if we meet their observations immediately with defensiveness or anger, we won't get any further toward solving the problem. They'll just shut down.

Once we know how we've offended, we must ask immediately and sincerely for forgiveness from our children. Even if our words weren't spoken with negative intent or were misunderstood, the offense is still real. We may try to explain what we really meant, but the bottom line is that we must still say, "I'm sorry that I hurt you with my words. Will you please forgive me?"

Keep in mind that to be sincere means we can't say something like, "*If* I've done anything wrong, please forgive me." That's not an admission of wrongdoing; it's an underhanded assertion of innocence.

Once we've asked for forgiveness, we need then and there to pray with our children so that in their presence we can ask for God's forgiveness, as well. Finally, we should go on to pray a blessing on them—if possible, one that specifically counteracts the curse we've just renounced.

When following these guidelines sincerely, I have no doubt that you'll see a change in both you and your child. Such is the power of the spoken word—to break the rule of evil, to heal, to forgive, and to bless.

The Lord watches over you —

the Lord is your shade at your right hand;

the sun will not harm you by day,

nor the moon by night.

The Lord will keep you from all harm —

he will watch over your life;

the Lord will watch over your coming and going

both now and forevermore.

PSALM 121:5-8 NIV

CHAPTER NINE

YOU CAN'T SAW SAWDUST

"Let bygones be bygones." "No use crying over spilled milk." "What's done is done." "You can't turn back the clock."

These are just a few of the clichés we tell ourselves for comfort when we think of all the things we wish we had done differently in life (or not done at all). And there is truth in each of these sayings, but they don't solve the problem. The apostle Paul taught us how we can deal with these things in our past: "But one thing I do," he wrote, "forgetting what is behind..." (Phil. 3:13 NIV). He didn't sit around mourning what he had done in the days before his conversion.

Nevertheless, Paul did more about his past than just put it behind him. He also used it as an inspiration for the future. He learned from his experiences, both good and bad, successes and failures. So he went on to affirm: "I press on...."

In light of Paul's words, take another look at the sayings just quoted. Though each attempts to encourage, none really succeed; they all stop short of what Paul said. Unlike Paul's statement, they fail to offer any hope for the future. Bygones really *are* bygones. What's done is done. And maybe you don't have to cry over spilled milk — but whether you cry or not, you still have to wipe it up.

Perhaps you've felt a bit guilty or remorseful as you've read this book because you didn't bless your kids when they were young and now they're not living at home anymore. Maybe you feel as if you "blew" it, not just in blessing your kids but in your parenting role in general. Or you might even be feeling a bit wistful about your own childhood and your relationship to your parents, because you know that as a child you didn't receive a blessing yourself.

If any of these things are true in your case, you may have been telling yourself, "Oh well, no use cryin' over spilled milk. It's too late. There's nothing I can do now."

That's not at all true. Actually, there's a great deal more you can do, even now. That's why I like another expression better than all the ones we mentioned. Some folks say, "You can't saw sawdust." Maybe not, but there's plenty you can make out of it.

MAKING PARTICLEBOARD OF THE PAST

For years lumber mills had few uses for the sawdust they were creating when they cut up their logs. Most of it just went to waste.

Then researchers discovered that by mixing the sawdust

with resin and compressing it, they could make a product that was stronger and less expensive than the original. Particleboard was born. As a result, sawdust is now being used extensively in all types of construction today.

A similar invention rescues waste scraps of leather. Did you know that there are no fewer than fifty different materials used in Bible covers? We cover the Word with pigskin, sheepskin, cowhide, and calfhide; durabond, leatherflex, skivertex, and kivar; chevo, croupon, rexine, and roncote, to name just a few. But by far the most popular deluxe binding for Bibles is called "bonded leather."

This material is made up of all the leftover scraps of genuine leather used in other Bible covers; the scraps are reprocessed and mixed with special resins. The result is a versatile new material that has all the qualities of the original leather but at a lower cost.

When you think of your past as a child or as a parent, think about that particleboard or the bonded leather. Have you considered how you might be able to make something new out of what's left over?

Perhaps you feel that the opportunity to be blessed by your parents or to bless your own children has passed and that there's nothing you can do to go back in time and change it all. As a youngster you may have been a model child or a rebel who turned your folks' hair gray. As a parent you may have used the time when your kids were young to

The past cannot be changed, but you can change the ongoing effects of what happened.

shape their character and values or you may have blown it completely. You may have just sailed through your childhood or your parenthood, blissfully unaware of all that could have been different, happy as a clam at high tide just to have survived.

In one sense, it really doesn't matter now. It's done. You're grown and out of your parents' home. Or your kids are grown and out of your home. The past cannot be changed, but you can change the ongoing effects of what happened. You can't saw sawdust, but you can make something of great value and usefulness out of it.

A SAWDUST MASTERPIECE

Years ago, I was admiring a beautiful sculpture that belonged to my sister-in-law and her husband. The artwork was the bust of a bald eagle entitled "In God We Trust."

The artist is Mario Fernandez, a Cuban refugee who entered the U.S. with nothing more than the clothes on his back and the American dream. In his native land, Mario had spent two years in prison as a young political dissenter. For him, the American dream represented everything that couldn't possibly be realized in Cuba. He had only been able to fulfill that dream through his strong faith in God. That's the reason behind the sculpture "In God We Trust."

Soon after admiring Mario's eagle, Mary and I received one as a gift from her sister and her husband. When I discovered what this gorgeous, hand-painted, limited edition bust of the bald eagle was created from, I was shocked. It was made from sawdust—sawdust mixed with resin, given value by the skill of an artist.

As I reflected on the nature of particleboard, bonded leather, and Mario's masterpiece, I saw the parallels between them and the possibilities of our own lives. In all of these cases, three things are necessary to create something new from scraps of the old:

1. An awareness of the value of the old, leftover scraps, no matter what their condition.

2. A resin to hold the material together.

3. A vision in the creator of what those scraps can become, whether the new creation is particleboard, bonded leather, a work of art, or a new relationship with our parents or children.

No matter what your past relationship with your parents or children has been, you can start with a clean slate today. Even if there was abuse, neglect, hypocrisy, or any number of destructive forms of behavior, those things are sawdust now, and it's up to you what you'll do with that sawdust. You can sweep it up and throw it out, saying, "Good riddance!" or you can say, "Look at this mess! What can I make out of this?"

God is the Master Artist who can look at those old, leftover scraps and see the finished product as a work of art, a new creation of precious value.

God is the Master Artist who can look at those old, leftover scraps and see the finished product as a work of art, a new creation of precious value. And God desires to take these "scraps" from our lives and mix them thoroughly with His "resin" until every piece is immersed in it. Then He can begin the process of creating works of art that bring glory and praise to Him.

What's the "resin" God uses to create something new? It's His Holy Spirit. As He fills us with His Spirit and we submit to His will, He's able to knead us until we're one with His Spirit and ready for His handiwork to be completed in our lives. This process brings healing to all the wounds caused by our parents' efforts or our own efforts to shape the original material.

IT'S NEVER TOO LATE

It's never too late to seek your parents' blessing or to give a blessing to your adult children. If you've never asked for your parents' blessing or given one to your own children before, start today.

Barbara Farmer worked with me in years past as an editor—and a really good one, I might add. [Editor's note: Thanks, Rolf!] Now, even though she has moved across the country with her family, she is once again working with me as my editor on this new edition of *The Family Blessing*. Recently she returned to Minneapolis, and when we met, she said, "I have something to tell you." Here is what she told me that day.

> *It's never too late to seek your parents' blessing or to give a blessing to your adult children.*

It was the morning after my uncle's funeral, and I woke up feeling not so refreshed. It had been several nights since I had slept well. So many things were weighing on my heart, mainly how my dad would handle the death of his younger brother, the "healthy one." This was just one of many recent circumstances wearing on Dad's defenses.

He'd always been a rock; a stoic, isolated heart. He cried once when his mom died; he hugged me on my wedding day, like a seawall hugs a wave. But when his brother got sick with inoperable cancer, chips and cracks skirted across his carefully laid stone. "It was supposed to be me," he said several times, referring to his own ailing health.

I gave Dad The Family Blessing *as a Christmas gift. I read this book years ago, and my husband and I began blessing our children right from their birth dates. This past year the book was again in my hands, and I just had to give it to Dad. When I arrived for the funeral a month later, he made it a point to tell me that he had finished the book.*

I was to return home the morning after the funeral and I only had a few hours left with my parents. I climbed out of bed and walked into the kitchen. Dad turned and immediately opened his arms and said, "There she is." He held me like the teddy bear I used to hold, and I cried. And he didn't let go right away, either.

A couple of hours later, it was time to say good-bye. I stopped him in the hall where we were alone, and we hugged again. Now was my chance. "Dad, may the Lord bless you and keep you, may He make His face shine upon you and be gracious unto you. May He lift up His countenance upon you and give you His peace. Amen."

"And the same for you," he said, sniffling.

"Dad, will you say it to me?" I asked.

He started and stumbled with emotion; I helped; he continued and finished with "...in Jesus name, amen." All this in one embrace.

The wall hasn't fallen completely yet, but there are pieces breaking away. It won't be easy; reconciliation doesn't happen in a day, but it's a start. I plan to send him another blessing soon...for his seventieth birthday.

Hurts and wounds can be healed. The resentment can be replaced by an attitude reflecting God's character. The heart of bitterness that destroys a life can become a heart of praise and gratefulness to God.

You may need to clear away a mound of garbage first—some things your parents dropped on you or you dropped on your children a long time ago, things no one ever bothered to pick up. If so, pick them up now. Go back to those parents or those kids and make it right. Ask them to forgive you for all the times you stumbled. Be specific. You know what those areas are that keep you from the kind of relationship you want with them.

You may feel that things are beyond saving. You might be thinking, *I really would like to do what you say, Rolf, but I know my kids (or my parents) wouldn't receive it. I know my spouse would laugh at me.* I doubt that anyone would laugh at you, especially if you have truly forgiven them in your heart. In any case, once you've sought and granted forgiveness, you cannot control their response. You can only control your own.

The most important part is for you to understand that God has forgiven you and that you only need to draw on that

As you walk in the light of that forgiveness, you'll radiate it to those around you.

forgiveness. Then you must also forgive yourself. As you walk in the light of that forgiveness, you'll radiate it to those around you. When they see it, they'll be drawn to it. And at that point they can receive your forgiveness and begin to be made whole, as well.

DOES IT WORK?

Some years ago when *The Family Blessing* first came out, Dr. James Dobson's Focus on the Family ministry used it as a premium and gave away over eleven thousand copies to their donors. Of course I was thrilled, but not nearly as thrilled as I was to hear the following story of one book recipient.

"Donnie" was a 22-year-old inmate at the state penitentiary in Manchester, Kentucky, where he was on death row and scheduled to die in the electric chair. He had been tried as an adult at the age of fifteen and found guilty of murder in the first degree.

Donnie was raised in a Christian home and knew the difference between right and wrong. However, like so many young kids, he saw a difference between what his parents taught him and how they lived. When he got a chance to make choices for himself, he chose to go with the wrong crowd and started doing things he knew were wrong. One thing just made it easier for him to do the next until the unthinkable happened and he ended up on death row.

His parents prayed for Donnie and asked God for guidance on what they could do to reach out to their son. They loved him and had long since forgiven him for his actions, but they didn't know what to do next. During this time his parents received a copy of *The Family Blessing* from Focus on the Family and were deeply challenged by the message. They decided to send it to their son in prison.

Donnie had done a lot of thinking during his incarceration. A lot! When he received the book from his parents, he was intrigued and decided to read it. A few days later his father called him. After talking for a long time, his dad told him that he wanted to bless him in Jesus' name. What happened next was God's grace at work. As his father blessed Donnie, both men wept and Donnie asked Christ into his heart.

Donnie made the effort to connect with Dan Straley, a friend of mine who had offered to be a contact person for readers of the first edition of the book. He told Dan about his life and about the phone call from his father and that he had given his life to Christ. As they ended their conversation, Donnie said to Dan, "You know, that's the first time my father has ever spoken to me like that" and they both wept.

Does blessing your children work? Absolutely! Is it ever too late to start? Absolutely not. Don't let another day pass without taking the time to hold your children in your arms as you pray for them and bless them. You will never regret it.

FORGIVENESS AND BLESSING GO HAND IN HAND

Does blessing your children work? Absolutely! Is it ever too late to start? Absolutely not.

In 1974, when Mary and I were still in Puerto Rico, I was asked by my pastor to be one of seven laymen to speak at the Good Friday service in our church. He said that each of us would have five minutes to speak on one of the "seven last words" of Christ on the cross (Matt. 27:46; Luke 23:34, 43, 46; John 19:26–30). When I asked him which of the seven words I was to speak on, he said, "You can take your pick. You're the first person I've asked." I scanned the list and selected the passage from Luke 23:34: "Father, forgive them; for they know not what they do" (KJV).

I had more than enough time to prepare for a five-minute talk. *Anyone can talk on forgiveness for five minutes,* I reasoned—so I didn't bother to think about it until the night before I was to speak. As I sat at my desk to scratch out a brief outline, nothing came to mind. I sat there for several hours reading and rereading the story of the crucifixion and commentaries on the subject. It was as though my mind had a lid on it. Nothing was coming. I finally gave it a rest.

Early the next morning, I returned to my office looking for some clarity in my thoughts. Nothing. I went to church early, thinking that maybe the surroundings and music might help. Nothing! Finally I looked at the bulletin, hoping to see my name at the bottom of the list so I could gain some insight from the other speakers.

Much to my chagrin, I was first on the program. I wondered, *Why am I first? Is it because he asked me first?* And then I saw it! I was first on the program because "Father, forgive them; for they know not what they do" was the first thing Jesus said from the cross. Before He said, "My God, my God, why hast thou forsaken me?" He declared to all around Him—persecutors, friends, families, the curious— "Father, forgive them; they don't know what they're doing." Before He said, "I thirst," He said, "Father, forgive them."

When I realized that Jesus' first concern was the forgiveness of those who were abusing Him, I couldn't wait to speak. No way was five minutes enough to share what I had just discovered.

By His example, Jesus showed us what He would do in and through us when we give Him the opportunity. The same Spirit that not only allowed Jesus to exhibit this forgiveness but also raised Him from the dead is the very Spirit that God wants to fill us with so we can

Experiencing God's forgiveness liberates us to begin to bless our families.

be conformed to His likeness. Then, and only then, can we truly know the power of forgiveness to set us and our offenders free from our past.

Experiencing God's forgiveness liberates us to begin to bless our families instead of cursing them. It opens the door to speak honestly to them without shame or guilt, because Jesus bore our shame and guilt on the cross.

If you're an adult who has never been blessed by your parents, go to them and request it. This will liberate both you and them to experience a new level of love and acceptance. If you're a parent of grown children, go to them and clear up the past. Then ask them to let you bless them. As you do, God will bless you all.

May our Lord Jesus Christ himself

and God our Father, who loved us and

by his grace gave us eternal encouragement

and good hope, encourage your hearts

and strengthen you in every good deed and word....

May the Lord direct your hearts

into God's love and Christ's perseverance....

Now may the Lord of peace himself

give you peace at all times and in every way.

The Lord be with all of you.

2 THESSALONIANS 2:16–17; 3:5, 16 NIV

CHAPTER TEN
CHERISH EVERY MOMENT

You know what amazes me? That I'll soon have a granddaughter in college. How is that possible? It seems like only recently that Carlton went off to college and not that much longer since I sat on his bed in Puerto Rico and began the practice of blessing him and Lisa. Maybe you feel the same way. Maybe you are looking back and thinking, "Wow! What happened? Where did all that time go? What would I do differently if I could live my life over again?"

Well, I am right there with you now myself. I am sure I would do many things exactly the same as I did the first time, but I would also do many things differently. For one thing, I have traveled all my adult life, which I have enjoyed immensely. I am nearly at my one-hundredth country and have been to all fifty states in the U.S., but to do that I have had to be away from my wife and kids a lot. Mary always put the best construction on my being gone, but I missed so many special occasions.

Today I have the joy of not only living near my two kids and their families but also working with my son and son-in-law in our publishing business. I love that. It also means that I can love on my five grandchildren and bless them.

But this has taken on a new significance for Mary and me recently. We have always taken it for granted that our children would be here long after we are gone, just like we did with our parents. Isn't that "God's will"?

But our loving Father sometimes has plans for us that we find very hard to understand. Sometimes the unthinkable happens and one of our children is called home before we are. It could happen through a senseless act of violence, combat in war, illness, an accident…. We never know what we will be asked to bear, and that uncertainty means we need to treasure every moment of every day we have with them, whether it is our children, grandchildren, our spouse, our loved ones, or our friends.

Recently our daughter, Lisa, her husband, Jason, and their four children all moved in with Mary and me. We were always hoping they would move back to Minneapolis and be near us, as they had spent the first ten years of their marriage in other parts of the country and the world. But that's not what brought them back. In the fall of 2008 their youngest child and only son, Von, was diagnosed with Acute Lymphoblastic Leukemia, or ALL for short. I wondered, "What is God doing letting three-year-olds get cancer?"

We have been told by the doctors at Children's Hospital in Minneapolis that kids with ALL today have an eighty-five percent chance of being cured. They have made amazing strides in the treatment of this disease in the past thirty years, and for this we are most grateful. We are believing that God's will is for Von to not only survive but to thrive and be a witness to God's grace in the world. But that is in His hands. At the time of this writing, Von is receiving chemo treatments, steroid doses, and a lot of therapy, and we are getting good reports from the doctors.

But what does one do differently when the uncertainty of life becomes reality?

But what does one do differently when the uncertainty of life becomes reality? Let me tell you, you immediately begin to cherish every day you have with that person — every moment. We have all become acutely aware of our need to bless Von and his healthy sisters in word and deed and to realize that it might not always be our privilege to do so.

Like many of you, Mary and I have family and friends who have suffered the ultimate pain through the loss of a child who never got to know what adult life is all about. I have asked three of these couples to share their stories here. There is joy in the knowledge that each of these three children were so very ready to stand in the presence of Almighty God, but there is also profound grief at their loss. Their stories are testimonies to God's over-and-above grace and love. As you read them, listen to what He is telling you about your own relationships, whether they are family, friends, or coworkers, and what you can do today to begin to cherish each day you have with them. I know your heart will be stirred by their experiences of loss and blessing. May God continue to bless them all for sharing their stories here.

Carol Garborg is married to Kjell, the youngest son of my older brother, Loren, and his wife, Clairice. Carol writes about their daughter in this memoir:

EMBRACING TODAY

Our newborn daughter was perfect. Silky brown hair. Stunning olive skin. The kind of eyelashes little girls wish for but little boys always seem to get. We named her Elise, oath of God. Thank you, Father, *I whispered. After the most difficult nine months of my life, everything was finally okay.*

But everything wasn't okay. Elise seemed uncharacteristically weak—low muscle tone, her pediatrician said—and she grew weaker. Within two months, my husband and I learned that Elise had a rare disease. Her nerve cells were slowly deteriorating, and she had less than a year to live.

That discovery introduced me to embracing the "now" of life. To love life for everything it is instead of regretting what wasn't. While other moms scheduled play dates and explored children's museums, Elise and I uncovered joys in more simple ways. Barely able to move, Elise spent her days in her infant seat. I sat cross-legged on the kitchen floor beside her, reading books and adding appropriate sound effects. "What does the baby chick say? Cheep, cheep." I'd push her stroller around a lake on crisp autumn days or trace her fingers over the veins of a brilliant maple leaf. Always she'd smile.

At night, when the smiles began to fade, I sang her the blessing from Psalms, "He who dwells in the shelter of the Most High will rest in the shadow of the Almighty." Rest, Elise, rest.

This was our reality and I cherished its simple joys.

This was our reality and I cherished its simple joys.

Thankfully most children will live full lives, not the short months Elise did. Embracing the "now-ness" of life, though, still applies. I often hear parents long for the day when their little one will finally—sigh—sleep through the night or start to crawl. I do understand. But too often what flavors each day disappears in the anticipation of what's to come. It's a little like longing for chocolate chip ice cream when butter pecan is still melting in your mouth. Each stage brings its own treasures, gifts that can be enjoyed for only that season. Throw your arms around today, and cherish the gifts it brings.

Dan and Joy Straley have been treasured friends since the early 70s when we lived in Puerto Rico. Dan writes about his daughter Marci.

GOD'S BENEDICTION

When Joy and I began our lives together nearly forty-two years ago, we wondered what the future would hold. It wasn't long before Lisa, our first daughter, arrived on the scene, which happened to be the Philippines where I was stationed. Our family expanded again after arriving at our next duty station, Morocco, where Marci joined us. Our third (and last) child, also a daughter, Andrea arrived after being stationed in Puerto Rico. We had the perfect family with three beautiful daughters. Over the years I enjoyed being the envy of many boys, followed by young men, who showed up with an eye for one of my girls. It was almost like being on autopilot on the perfect journey through life.

During this wonderful chapter of our lives, I had the extraordinary privilege of praying God's blessing over my girls during significant events in their lives. The blessing from Numbers 6 (the priestly prayer of Aaron), was always delivered the same way and the result was always the same: tears of gratitude and joy for the peace God gave in the middle of whatever storm was brewing.

In the later months of Marci's senior year she was diagnosed with pancreatic cancer, and our happy, relatively bump-free ride came to a sudden and frightening halt. She was 18 years old. My thoughts went back to several years prior when I opted out of a career that took me away from my girls far too often, and I wept with thanks at God's direction.

Four years of chemotherapy, multiple operations, congestive heart failure, and untold stints in the hospital followed, all preceded with "the blessing" as we sought to put God ahead of our own limited perspective.

I was at work on the afternoon of February 4, 1993, when I received a page from a doctor in California where Marci was receiving treatment. "Marci is gravely ill, and you need to get here as soon as possible if you are to see her alive." Joy and I caught a flight a couple of hours later and arrived late that evening. When we got to the hospital, Marci was barely conscious but knew we were there.

All night Joy sang and spoke Scripture to Marci while I prayed and made many trips back and forth across the room, ending up at her bedside to be with her. But it became apparent that Marci was heaven-bound. We noticed that her breathing had become very labored, and we went to her side, Joy on one side and me on the other. Then Marci missed a breath and Joy shrieked, "Get the doctor!"

"Let her go, Joy," I said. I watched my wife's expression change from keeping Marci here with us at all costs to the most

> *Every day is precious with time enough to love deeply.*

painful expression of faith and selflessness I have ever witnessed. We both released her.

"Marci, the Lord bless you and keep you, the Lord make His face to shine upon you and be gracious to you; the Lord lift up His countenance upon you and give you peace. In the name of the Father, Son, and Holy Spirit I pray. Amen." And she was gone — safe in the outstretched arms of the One who had held her hand the entire journey.

In twenty-two short years God weaved a beautiful tapestry that was my daughter's life. I've learned some extraordinary lessons from this journey: Every day is precious, with time enough to love deeply; Marci's death was not the final crushing blow but the most profound life-changing event I will ever witness; the light in Marci's lamp has not gone out — it is the dawn; and finally, God works best with broken hearts. He is the Potter. In His hands I find life and provision. And Marci knows complete healing in His hands.

Thanks, Rolf, for sharing The Family Blessing *with me over thirty-five years ago. For my family and me, it has been God's benediction.*

Mike and Gwen Bonnema have been a special part of our lives since they graduated from college in the spring of 1976. They share the story of their son Jon.

BLESSING JON BONNEMA

Jonathon "Jon-Bon" Bonnema came into our lives in August 1987, and though he came as a surprise package, he truly lived up to the meaning of his name, which is "God's gracious gift." We had learned several years earlier while raising our older children about the power of blessing, and so it fit right in to begin blessing Jon from the moment we first knew he was coming.

As a father I always enjoy praying blessings over my children, but it became even more enjoyable as they grew and we could see their personalities and unique qualities develop. For Jon, the two traits that stood out were an extreme quietness whenever anyone outside of our immediate family was around, and the ability to be just hilarious for the rest of us all the time. Quite honestly, at the time I did not know how God could use those two strong traits of quietness and comedy for His glory. I probably would have picked out different things for my son, but that seemed to be who he was, so I began to bless his ability to be funny and asked God to make him a strong leader even if he was going to be quiet.

By the time Jon was in sixth grade, I found myself quite frustrated that he stayed so quiet. Even though he seemed very confident in himself and he seemed to not have anything against me, he wouldn't open up. I remember missing a basketball game and asking him how it went. He was happy to tell me they won and how well his teammates did. When I finally asked how he did, he said "Fine" and walked away. Later his teammates came over all excited about the fact that Jon had made twenty-three points and had a buzzer beater from three-quarter court.

I wondered why Jon had not wanted to share his successes with me, so I asked the Lord what I was doing wrong. The Lord seemed to say, "Mike, the way I made him makes him think you are blowing smoke when you compliment him. It is important for Jon to see himself as I see him." From that time on I tried to compliment him through the Lord. My blessing would be something like, "Hey, Jon, do you know why the Lord wants you to be a leader? Because He sees you as a man of great integrity. Jon, I bless you in Jesus' name to be a great man of integrity." Another time I asked Jon if he knew why the Lord made him so funny. His response was no, so I said, "Jon, your heavenly Father knows that you are very creative, and He knows you will use that humor to build up other kids. Father, in Jesus' name I bless Jon to use his humor to bring healing to his friends."

The last time Gwen and I had an opportunity to bless our son was on March 24, 2006. Jon and two teammates were on their way to school the day prior to join the rest of their basketball team to go to the state tournament. They never made it. A terrible car accident took the life of Jon's good friend Adam Mikelson instantly. Jon was airlifted to the hospital, where we were joined by two hundred people who spent the day with us fighting the fight of faith, believing and waiting for a miracle. As painful as our day was, the love of the Lord was never more evident to us than through all our friends.

Early the next morning, with about twenty-five family and friends around Jon's bed, a doctor walked into our room and told us about some tests they had run, concluding with the only words I remember: "I am sorry, Mr. and Mrs. Bonnema, but your son is legally brain-dead. There is nothing you or we can do."

In looking back at that moment, I am so thankful that the Lord had helped both Gwen and me turn our times of blessing into a constant habit, because that is the first thing we did when we got the news. We turned to Jon and laid hands on his still-beating heart and said, "Jon, from the moment we knew you were coming into this world, we loved you and blessed you. You have meant so much to us, and you have blessed us. We did not choose for you to go to heaven now, but we choose to give you our blessing as you go. We love you; we will always love you. We will see you again. We bless you in the name of the Father, the Son, and the Holy Spirit." With that we sang and worshipped our Lord as Jon met his Savior.

We spent one more day at the hospital while LifeSource worked to find people who were ready to receive Jon's heart and many other organs. On the quiet ride home I began to think about Jon's life. Did he accomplish all that God intended? How did he impact people? What was his secret life? Was it what I had hoped it to be, or would I learn about bad decisions he had made? What was his real legacy? The answers became the avenue that God used to show us His grace.

From the stories we heard from Jon's friends, he did not seem to just use his humor to make people laugh, but to get into their hearts and help them see themselves as God saw them. We heard many times in different ways that Jon had taught them how to really live.

I had a number of dramatic encounters that brought me much more joy than I could have ever anticipated. One example was when I found a picture that Gwen had taken on one of her nature hikes with the kids when Jon was four years old. In the picture, Jon was probably throwing leaves in the air, but to me it looked like he was praising God with all he had. In an instant I knew that on the day the picture was taken, the Lord knew how many days Jon would live, and our Lord was okay with that and that Jon's work on Earth was done. I was instantly at peace and tremendously happy that Jon experienced a life that was well-lived for his Savior.

> *I am so thankful that I had people teach me the power of blessing.*

Gwen tells about how Jon's friends came to our house after he died, individually or *in small groups. Not really knowing how to handle the tragedy, they would just talk and talk. She would tell the kids that we wanted them to develop the gifts God gave them but that nothing was more important than their decision to follow Christ.*

I am so thankful that I had people teach me the power of blessing. Without it, I could have missed some of the unique qualities of my son, and I could have stayed disappointed with him in some ways even though I loved him very much. Instead I was able to partner with my heavenly Father to help Jon be Jon, just the way he was created to be.

I share these stories with the hope that God will challenge you to start cherishing each moment you have with your loved ones; that you will bless them with your words, your actions, and your heart in every encounter; and that you will grow deeper in God's love and blessing as you do so.

My father used to say that he always wanted to "keep short accounts" with everyone. We knew instinctively what he meant by the way he lived and the way he loved. He didn't want to leave anything unfinished when he left us. Part of that legacy was that neither he nor my mother ever said good-bye to us without a kiss on the cheek and an "I love you" whispered in the ear. In fact, that was the last thing Dad did before he died.

Look at the gifts of relationships that God has allowed you to develop and cherish them today. Begin to "express praise, to speak well of" your friends and family and watch what He does both in you and in your relationships with them...and give it time to grow.

Now to Him who is able to keep you from stumbling,

and to make you stand in the presence of His glory

blameless with great joy,

to the only God our Savior, through Jesus Christ our Lord,

be glory, majesty, dominion and authority,

before all time and now and forever. Amen.

JUDE 1:24–25 NASB

CHAPTER ELEVEN
EXPANDING THE CIRCLE

What about all those "OPKs" (Other People's Kids) out there? Who will bless them? Someone once said that we may be the only Bible some people ever read. We may also be the only one ever to speak a blessing on some people. Do we dare pass up the opportunity?

Blessing children as defined in this book is not limited to our own children. It's not even limited to children. It extends to include the entire "human family."

Jesus' own example was one of blessing other people's kids.

Jesus' own example was one of blessing other people's kids. It was typical of Jesus to take the children in His arms, place His hands on them, and bless them (Mark 10:16). No doubt kids often surrounded Him—not only because they felt comfortable being near Him but also because they knew He had a blessing in store for them.

Grandparents are the most obvious folks who are in a position to bless children, especially their children's children.

My grandfather was a classic example of a blesser. He loved kids; he had fourteen children and twenty-eight grandchildren. We always loved to be with Grandpa. He was continually doing something to make us laugh. And best of all, when we were gathered in the living room, Grandpa would reach into his pocket, jingle his change, and start tossing coins on the carpet. We would all dive into a pile to get our share. It was a kind and loving "blessing" to demonstrate his delight in the little ones around him. Each child knew he had Grandpa's approval, which was important to him.

A relationship with grandparents is extremely important in the self-esteem and character development of a child.

Instead of dispensing coins to his grandchildren, my dad always carried in his shirt pocket "kokky" — broken pieces of hard candy. Before his grandkids could walk or talk, they understood that Grandpa had "kokky." They knew where to find it and that my dad had an unlimited supply. They simply had to crawl up on his lap and dig in.

A relationship with grandparents is extremely important in the self-esteem and character development of a child. Studies suggest that children who have been raised near their grandparents and spend time with them have a heightened sense of security and well-being.

Recently I heard of a program developed to involve grandparents in the lives of children of single mothers. Research by the group sponsoring this program concurred with other studies concerning the value of the presence of a grandfather in the life of a young boy raised by a single mom. This was especially evident for boys age ten to fifteen.

If the presence and social involvement of a grandparent can positively impact children in such environments, consider the benefits those children receive when that grandparent actively blesses them. That blessing can include both a verbal, hands-on-the-head, straight-out-of-Numbers 6:24–26 blessing as well as other simple blessings: the spoken words "God bless you," a loving caress, a kind word, an encouraging smile, an understanding nod, a listening ear, a forgiving kiss, a comforting shoulder. All these are accepting and approving signs of interest in the child.

Grandparents often have two important qualities to contribute in building relationships with children: time and patience. So it's wonderful when they choose to invest that precious commodity in their grandchildren.

Grandparents often have two important qualities: time and patience.

My grandmother had a rare quality that was a great blessing for youngsters: serenity. She had the ability to take whatever life brought her with grace, to praise God in both good and bad times, to remain faithful during times of struggle, and to serve others cheerfully without complaining, even when their needs might not have been as great as her own. She certainly earned the title of saint if anyone ever did.

"Gramma," as we called her, came from Norway as a teenager and settled in Superior, Wisconsin. She married Lars Roholt and gave birth to her first seven children at home over a ten-year period. During one four-year stretch of terrible grief, the first-, fourth-, and sixth-born children (all boys) died: one of scarlet fever at age six, one of typhoid fever at age three, and the last of dehydration at the age of six months. In addition, each of the other four children also nearly died of scarlet fever.

Around the time the sixth child was born, Gramma was so severely crippled with arthritis that she could not comb her own hair for the pain and had to crawl to climb stairs. Yet no one ever heard her complain. She gave her grief to God.

Gramma's arthritis improved significantly when she and her family moved away from the cold, damp conditions around Lake Superior. She soon became a leader in her church. She was a blessing to everyone she met. She also gave birth to seven more children!

By the time she had reached her early fifties, Gramma's

arthritis had returned. For the remainder of her life, she was in constant pain. Yet the most negative remark I ever heard her say regarding her condition was that it kept her from doing more for others. She said, in her thick Norwegian accent, "If I yust had two good legs, I vould run and yump like a spring shicken."

One day when Gramma was ninety-two years old and living with my parents, she hobbled out from her bedroom on her walker and said to my mother, "Ya, Blanche. You know, I vas reading in dis magazine, and I found a vord dat tells yust da type of person dat I am." The word was *optimist*.

She was that all right, and much more. She was also an overcomer, one who considered the needs of others greater than her own, and she was always looking for ways to share the victory she knew so well in Jesus. She was a "blesser" in every way.

Grandparents have a multitude of opportunities to bless grandchildren.

Grandparents have a multitude of opportunities to bless grandchildren, and their role in a child's life is vital. They often have the time and character qualities that children need.

No parent, or even two parents, can meet the constant needs of a child all the time. The need for a child to be blessed with a parent's regular attention, approval, and goodwill is real and extremely difficult to fill consistently by most parents. So finding other supportive adults to enrich your child's life can provide blessings to both of you.

Caring adult Christians can become "blessing activists." Look for those to whom you can give a thoughtful, encouraging word. The world is full of opportunities to give a sincere, loving compliment, to say a word to brighten a child's day, or to show them that you care.

It doesn't take much time to express a blessing or two on a daily basis. Just consider the places you go where you could encounter an opportunity to bless a child. Ask God to show you what you can do to start blessing those "OPKs."

HE IS ABLE

The biblical gift of blessing was not limited to blessing children; people of all ages should receive the favor and power of God. We all have a child within. If that child was never blessed, it's still looking for the blessing. The search doesn't end when we become adults.

Recently, Rick was a guest in our home. He is a friend of my daughter, Lisa, and her husband, Jason, and he came to Minnesota just to pray for their three-year-old son, Von, who is battling Acute Lymphoblastic Leukemia at the time of this writing. While Rick was here he shared his testimony with us before our time of prayer for Von. I was amazed at his story.

Rick grew up in a very religious Catholic home. So ardent was he about his faith that he wanted to become a priest for many years. Then as a teenager he discovered girls and decided that he could not become a priest after all. His new pursuit led him down a very slippery slope that changed everything in his life. As he experienced each new thing—girls, drugs, alcohol, money—he drifted further and further from his roots until he finally declared himself an atheist.

As the years went by, Rick continued to chase after the excitement and allure that came with his new lifestyle; but instead of fulfillment, he felt more and more empty. One day he found himself crying out to God to take him back and forgive him for all he had done. He found a beautiful Christian woman who became his wife, and they soon began building a family.

But with all the baggage from his past, there was still a struggle to make a wholehearted commitment to God. Even then, his wife walked faithfully with him, loving him and believing that he would come to truly understand the saving grace of God. After a season in the wilderness, he made it through and has dedicated himself to the Lord and his family for many years.

After Rick prayed passionately for Von, each of the others present joined in prayer, including each of Von's three young sisters. It was a most special time. As the evening came to an end, I felt I should bless Rick. I couldn't get the blessing from the end of the book of Jude out of my mind. Finally, I stood and walked over to where Rick was seated, placed my hands on his head, and prayed for him. Then I quoted the blessing from Jude 1:24–25 (KJV). "Now unto Him who is able to keep you from falling, and to present you faultless before the presence of his glory with exceeding joy, to the only wise God our Savior, be glory and majesty, dominion and power, both now and forever. Amen."

Rick shook with sobs as he received this affirmation of what God had done in his life and said afterward that this was going to be his life verse.

I have thought of this blessing in a whole new light since this time with Rick. When I look closer at this blessing, I see that the core is "now unto Him...be glory and majesty, dominion and power, both now and forever." That is what I can offer up to God. The rest of the blessing is the extraordinary gift that God has given us. Jesus is "able to keep us from falling," and He is "able to...present us faultless." *Faultless!* And finally, He does all this "with *exceeding joy*" as he presents us "to the only wise God who is our Savior"! It's no wonder that we give Him glory and majesty, dominion and power. So great is our God! So worthy to be blessed and praised!

Countless people, whether children or adults, are waiting for someone to speak God's blessing into their lives.

It may be a brother or sister who needs a blessing, or perhaps a friend or coworker. Most of us have a number of close contacts with adults outside our family whose ongoing relationships could provide the opportunity for speaking a blessing.

Countless people, whether children or adults, are waiting for someone to speak God's blessing into their lives. The possibilities for blessing are endless. Start today.

May the God of hope fill you with all joy

and peace as you trust in him,

so that you may overflow with hope

by the power of the Holy Spirit....

The God of peace be with you all. Amen.

ROMANS 15:13, 33 NIV

CHAPTER TWELVE

BLESSING AS A WAY OF LIFE

Everybody loved my father—everybody, that is, except Mr. and Mrs. Aune. They were neighbors on the lake where we lived for thirteen years. It wasn't a personal thing. At least it didn't start out that way.

Twenty years before we moved into the house next to theirs, the Aunes had a severe crossing of wills with a member of their church. Rather than resolve that conflict, they became extremely bitter—not just toward that one member or even the entire membership of their church. No, they were bitter toward anyone who attended church anywhere. And they told anyone who would listen.

The Aunes were in their midsixties when we met. When they learned that we were Christians, they wanted nothing to do with us or our faith. We tried to honor their wishes, but God had other plans.

Our home was on a lake on several acres of land, giving our dog Shultz ample room to run. But somehow it was never room enough, so he often visited the Aunes' yard, as well.

Shultz's trespassing especially bothered Mrs. Aune. She showed her frustration by shouting various things at him, none of which he understood. She even notified the town constable about Shultz. We tried to keep Shultz home, but when a boat pulling a water skier came close to our shoreline, a ball and chain could not have held him.

The day finally came when Mrs. Aune and Shultz had a showdown. She was out in her yard digging dandelions, using a picker with a five-foot wooden handle on one end and a sharp, twin-pointed blade on the other. When Shultz came flying through her yard, she wound up like a baseball pitcher and let the lethal weapon fly. Fortunately for Shultz, she was out of practice and the lance sailed harmlessly over his back.

With his heart overflowing with compassion, my father replied, "My dear Mrs. Aune... God bless you."

Within minutes, Mrs. Aune was pounding on our door. Having observed the encounter through our window, my dad offered to greet our visitor. The next few moments I'll never forget. When my dad opened the door, there was Mrs. Aune, literally bouncing up and down with rage like some plastic wind-up toy.

For what seemed like an eternity, Mrs. Aune screamed at my dad at the top of her lungs. When she ran out of words, she stood there sputtering like an old motor. Finally she ran out of gas and stopped. With his heart overflowing with compassion, my father replied, "My dear Mrs. Aune, I am so sorry that we have upset you. Will you ever forgive us? We'll try not to let it happen again. God bless you, Mrs. Aune." For a brief moment, she stood there in stunned silence. She was defenseless. Then she spun on her heels and charged back across the yard.

For several weeks we didn't see Mr. and Mrs. Aune, and Dad became concerned. Their lawn, usually nicely kept, was overgrown and in desperate need of mowing. So after considerable prodding from Dad, my brother and I were finally convinced to mow their lawn. We were about fourteen and sixteen years old at the time, and this wasn't how we had planned to spend a warm summer day at the lake. It was an all-day job to mow and rake their large lawn. But we did it, however reluctantly.

No sign of life appeared in the Aune house while we worked, but we knew they were home. Two weeks later, my brother and I again protested as Dad asked us to mow their lawn. This time we saw Mrs. Aune peeking from behind the curtains.

Two more weeks passed when Dad looked over at the Aunes' lawn and said, "Well, boys?" We knew what that meant. This time, just as we were finishing, Mrs. Aune came outside carrying a tray with a large glass of lemonade for both of us. She thanked us for mowing her lawn and explained that her husband, Al, had not been well. We told her we were sorry and were glad to help in any way we could. Later that fall, Mrs. Aune called. "Can you come quickly? Al is very ill." Mom and Dad rushed to their home. Mrs. Aune took them to the bedroom where her husband lay. They talked with Mr. Aune about his illness, his past with the church, the state of his soul, and the redeeming blood of Christ that could make him clean again. Mr. Aune listened, thanked them, and asked them to please come back.

Over the next few weeks, Dad and Mom visited the Aunes several times. Finally, the day came when both Mr. and Mrs. Aune prayed to receive Christ as their Savior. I can still remember my parents' joy when they told us the story.

Much of what I've learned about blessing I learned from my father.

Two weeks later, Mr. Aune went to be with the Lord. Mrs. Aune joined our church, soaking up everything she could. The following summer she was baptized in Lake Wissota. She grew in her faith and became a close friend of our family. Then a few years later she joined her husband. What would have happened to Mr. and Mrs. Aune if my dad had responded to her in a harsh way that summer afternoon? Instead, God used a soft answer, a kind word, a loving deed, and a blessing to expand His kingdom here on earth.

Dad's response to Mrs. Aune that day was not an isolated instance of Christlikeness. Much of what I've learned about blessing I learned from my father. He not only was a man who knew how to bless people, he used the blessing as a way of life.

The biblical portrait of King David shows us another man who knew blessing as a way of life. In fact, of the many recorded uses in the Bible of some form of the word *bless*, more than seventy are attributed to David. And on one particular occasion, when he regained the Ark of the Lord from his enemies, this king displayed a pattern that we might all want to imitate. At that time David spoke a blessing in three directions. We read that he blessed God for His goodness, saying, "Blessed be the Lord, the God of Israel, from everlasting even to everlasting" (1 Chron. 16:36 NASB). He also blessed all the people around him: "When David finished offering the burnt offerings, he blessed the people in the name of the Lord" (1 Chron. 16:2). Finally, he gave the blessing to his family: "Then all the people departed each to his house, and David returned to bless his household" (1 Chron. 16:43).

As we read the many stories about David in Scripture, we read about someone who seems to have been continually blessing God, blessing his family, and blessing the people. His son Solomon was evidently so impressed with the example that he followed the pattern his father had established

(1 Kings 8:12–15). No wonder, then, that King David, the man of blessing, was called a man after God's own heart, who would do everything God wanted him to do (Acts 13:22).

A single point of commitment in establishing a habit that takes only minutes provides a lifetime of benefits.

The family blessing spoken regularly over kids is just the center of a circle of influence that can widen to include our interactions in all relationships. Beginning the process may seem like a daunting challenge. But the beauty of it all is that change begins with the first blessing. A single point of commitment in establishing a habit that takes only minutes provides a lifetime of benefits. When we start by learning to be faithful in little things, we can go on to become faithful in greater things (Matthew 25:21).

A HEART CLEANSING

Blessing our children and others around us is like so many other disciplines of the Christian life. It can all too easily be swept under the rug and neglected. The problem with our "under-the-rug" tendency is that we soon end up with so much there, both good and bad, that we don't know where to start to clean it all up. That's normal. It happens to all of us. Ultimately, we have to deal with what's under the rug. It's better to start now than to wait until later. It's a lie to think that having garbage in your life is okay as long as you keep it hidden.

I once went through a particularly difficult time spiritually. I had so much garbage under the carpets, in the corners, and in every closet of my life that it was starting to spill over into noticeable areas. When things finally got desperate, I cried out to God for help.

He began a wonderful heart cleansing. He walked through every room of my heart, shining the gentle light of His Holy Spirit into each dark corner. There was no condemnation or judgment, just the knowledge that everything was going to be okay.

I asked, "Lord, how will we ever clean this mess up?" And He responded, *Don't worry about that. We'll take it one room at a time.* Then I was reminded of the comfort in Paul's words to the Philippians: "Being confident of this very thing, that he which hath begun a good work in you will perform it until the day of Jesus Christ" (1:6 KJV).

On that particular day when God began this cleansing work in me, an article in the local paper caught my eye. The story was about an old, stately mansion in St. Paul, Minnesota, that had been the pride and joy of its original owners. Through years of rough use and poor maintenance, the home had fallen into disrepair. Finally it was abandoned and slated to be demolished.

Only days before the scheduled demolition, a young couple drove by and, looking beyond the obvious, saw what it could become. They decided to buy it for restoration. An unusual agreement was finally reached: The city sold them the mansion for one dollar on the condition that they move in on the day of closing. The couple agreed. The house was a filthy, rat-infested, broken-windowed disaster, fit only to be destroyed—to everyone, that is, but the new owners. After a three-year renovation, the home reflected the character of the young couple in every room. When the reporter who initially interviewed them inquired how they managed to tackle this job, they replied that after walking through each room, noting what needed to be done, they decided to finish one room at a time until the task was completed.

We are all a work in progress, being remodeled by His Spirit.

I'm deeply grateful that God in His wisdom deals with us that way. We are all a work in progress, being remodeled by His Spirit. That should give us hope for the changes taking place in our lives and the lives of our family members.

As you've read this book, I pray that God has spoken to you. Perhaps He's made you aware of some lumps under your carpet and offered to help you clean them up.

Let Him start cleaning now. Just as the newly remodeled mansion reflected the character of the couple who bought it, let God begin to reflect His character in your life through His remodeling efforts.

START WHERE YOU ARE

Maybe some of *The Family Blessing* rings true, while other points don't relate to your experience at all. That's as it should be. It's like going through a smörgåsbord: More than likely everything tastes good, but not all of it appeals to you at once. So take what you can benefit from now and begin to put it to work in your life.

Start with the part that is most important to you. Perhaps you need restoration with the parents who never blessed you. Maybe your concern is forgiveness from your children who are grown and gone. Maybe God is emphasizing to you to speak well of others. Whatever it is, start there.

It's not important to understand everything before you do anything. Begin to apply the principles of blessing by starting *where you are*. Apply what you do understand and make some mistakes along the way rather than wait until everything is clear. It will all become clear in time.

Meanwhile, in the beginning, don't be afraid of "botching things up." Others will be supportive and eager to help. If your heart is right in what you do, God will make up the difference.

Start to bless today! The blessing carries with it rich rewards that begin to accrue immediately. The apostle Paul said, "The Lord has assigned to each his task. I planted the seed, Apollos watered it, but God made it grow...and each will be rewarded according to his own labor" (1 Cor. 3:5–6, 8 NIV). God has assigned to each of us the task of blessing others, and He will give the reward.

> *The blessing carries with it rich rewards that begin to accrue immediately.*

HERITAGE: THE GREATEST REWARD OF BLESSING

Perhaps the greatest reward of blessing is the heritage it allows us to leave our children—the kind of heritage my father left for my brothers and me.

Dad was a giant in my eyes. He was a hard worker and a good provider. And he showed his love for my mother and his boys. Every greeting to us included a hug and an "I love you." He never raised his voice to my mother, and I never heard them argue or fight.

As a child, every morning when I stumbled out of my bedroom, I would see Dad lying on the couch reading his Bible and praying. His one overwhelming motivation in life was to see his three boys come to know and love God with all their hearts.

Dad and Mom prayed together daily. Their prayers included the request that each son would find a wife who loved him and shared his faith and commitment to the Lord. Those prayers have been wonderfully answered.

When Mary and I were married, we received many beautiful gifts and loving wishes. One gift in particular that we treasure to this day was the Scripture verse my parents gave us as a lifelong blessing on our marriage: "And be ye kind one to another, tenderhearted, forgiving one another, even as God for Christ's sake hath forgiven you" (Ephesians 4:32 KJV).

Dad kept short accounts, whether it was in business or in personal relationships. One of my favorite stories he used to tell us kids concerned a little girl in Norway who asked her mother when Jesus was coming back.

> *"And be ye kind one to another, tenderhearted, forgiving one another, even as God for Christ's sake hath forgiven you."*
>
> Ephesians 4:32 KJV

"Well," her mother told her, "we don't know when that will be. It could be at any time."

The daughter thought for a moment and said, "Then, Mother, it's pretty important that we have our suitcase packed, isn't it?"

Dad's bags were always packed. He was always ready to go.

On a cold January morning in 1985, Mom and Dad rose early, well before dawn as always, and went to their favorite chairs to read and pray together. Besides the Bible, Dad's favorite book was a devotional by the Norwegian author Frederick Wisloff called *Rest a While*. He had read it through countless times in both Norwegian and English. The following is the passage he read that morning:

Like a weaver I have rolled up my life;
He cuts me off from the loom;
from day to night Thou dost bring me to an end.

ISAIAH 38:12

A human life is likened unto a tapestry that is to be woven. Day by day the shuttle moves back and forth, and the tapestry grows. As thread is laid upon thread, the design begins to emerge. A thread is such a tiny thing. And yet the whole tapestry is made up of such threads. If some threads are improperly woven, the whole design will be marred.

A day appears so small and insignificant. And yet, each day is a part of my whole life. If each single day is lived improperly and carelessly, what will this do to the design of my life? When the tapestry is finished, it is rolled up, and the ends of the threads are cut off. Then it can be woven no more. It is put away until the day when it is placed on exhibition and judged.

Dear God, grant that the tapestry of my life may be properly woven. I give Thee the shuttle. Do with me as Thou wilt, if only Thy image may some day be the design in my tapestry when the threads of my life are cut off, and the tapestry is judged.[1]

When Dad finished reading this, he wept as he poured out his heart to his Father in prayer. Dad rarely cried—except in prayer. When he prayed, he was often so overwhelmed by God's love that he would weep with gratitude. This day he was as grateful as ever for all that God had done.

As Dad prayed, he interceded, as always, for his wife, his boys, and their families. He then prayed for himself, that an improperly woven thread would not mar the tapestry of his life. He prayed that God would cleanse him of all areas of sin in his life, and that he would be clean as he stood before Him.

That evening my brother and his wife ate supper with my parents. As they sat around the table afterward, Dad said, "You know, I have been dreaming a lot lately, and it is usually the same dream. I see myself as part of a vast multitude of believers standing before the throne of God, and we are all worshipping the Lord. Sometimes I look around at the people, and I recognize some as friends. I then realize that all of these friends have died. Do you think there is anything to these dreams?"

My brother and his wife didn't quite know what to say. Two days earlier, Dad had given a friend a hug and said to him, "You know, Terry, I just long to be with my Lord, don't you?" So they wondered about what all this might mean.

Later that evening, after a bowl of ice cream and the evening news, Dad gave Mom a tender hug, told her how much he loved her, breathed out a sigh, and was gone—gone to be with the Lord he loved and served. He was seventy-eight.

Not a day goes by without a reminder of Dad. For instance, when my son was going through some times of searching and questioning his faith, I felt I should visit him at college. As we talked well into the night, he reminisced.

"Dad," he recalled, "four years ago when Grandpa was alive, I stopped by to see him and Grandma. We talked for a while, and as I was about to leave, I gave them both a hug and a kiss and told them I loved them. Then Grandpa said,

In a powerful sense Dad's whole life was a blessing.

'Carlton, you know, my deepest desire for you is that you know and love the Lord with all your heart.'

"You know, Dad," Carlton said, "those are the last words Grandpa ever said to me." We both cried.

Several weeks after Dad went to be with the Lord, Mom was going through his belongings. Tucked away was a letter to his three sons and our families. It was written in his own hand, and it reminisced about his childhood in Norway, meeting our mother, and his love for the Lord. Before the letter ended, he made certain we knew what was beating most in his heart for us:

> *Now in closing I just want you to know that we love you all — children, your spouses, grandchildren, and great-grandchildren. We pray for you and mention your name before the throne of grace every day. Our most sincere prayer is that we may all meet home in that glory land someday. Stay close to Jesus, and He will stay close to you. [The Lord] says, "Fear not, for I am with you. Be not dismayed for I am your God; I will help you and strengthen you and uphold you with the right hand of my righteousness"* (Isaiah 41:10 PARAPHRASE).

In these words, Dad gave us his blessing. In a powerful sense his whole life was a blessing. He knew the heart of God, and he desired that his three boys and their families would also know the heart of God. To that end he committed his life — a commitment that my mother shared until she went to join my dad at age ninety-four.

What is the family blessing? It's an active commitment to our children's highest good, that they might know and love the Lord their God with all their hearts.

Perhaps the story of my father's last day can help us consider the big picture of our lives. Each little word, each interaction with our kids is a thread that joins many others to form the fabric of our children's character. What will that fabric be?

Each attitude we cultivate is a stitch in the tapestry of our own lives. What will be the final pattern of that tapestry when we one day present it to God for His approval? If we learn, as my father did, to make blessing a way of life, our children's fabric will be strong. The tapestry of a godly example we leave as their heritage will be beautiful. Then truly the Lord will bless us and keep us; the Lord will make His face to shine upon us and be gracious to us; the Lord will lift up His countenance upon us and give us peace. For what greater blessing could we ask?

> *The family blessing is an active commitment to our children's highest good.*

START PRACTICING THE FAMILY BLESSING

1. Now is the time to start blessing your children. It's never too early for them to begin receiving the benefits of being blessed. Refer to this book once a month or until the message of blessing becomes a personal passion in your life. Take full advantage of the time you have—start today!

2. Find a consistent time to bless your family. There are no right or wrong times or frequencies—simply pray and seek God about what is best for your family. Remember, structure and consistency are important, especially to young children.

3. Seek God's wisdom on what biblical or biblically inspired blessing is right for your family and begin to use it. Remember, all the blessings don't have to be the same every time.

4. Explain to your children what a blessing is and why you are speaking it over them. Use a meaningful touch (a hug, a hand on a shoulder, etc.) when blessing them.

5. Supplement the blessing with a prayer over your children and expect to see amazing results!

6. Share with others the rewards of blessing. Explain to aunts, uncles, grandparents, and friends what you are doing and encourage them to practice blessings in their own lives. Encourage them to either use the blessings provided in *The Family Blessing* or establish their own biblically inspired blessing.

7. Tell your pastor what you are doing and ask him or her to pray for you as you begin.

8. Look for opportunities to bless others (neighbors, coworkers, friends, etc.). Adapt a lifestyle of blessing.

9. Share how practicing *The Family Blessing* has changed your life. You are invited to visit my Web site: www.rolfgarborg.com.

Chapter 1

1. Larry Christenson, *The Christian Family* (Minneapolis: Bethany Fellowship, 1970), 195–197.

Chapter 2

1. Larry G. Lenning, *Blessing in Mosque and Mission* (Pasadena: William Carey Library, 1980), 74.

2. John R. Kohlenberger III and James A. Swanson, *New International Version Exhaustive Concordance*, 2nd ed. (Grand Rapids: Zondervan, 1999).

Chapter 3

1. *Fiddler on the Roof* by Jerry Bock, Sheldon Harnick, and Arnold Perl. Music and lyrics copyright © 1964 by Sunbeam Music Corp. Used with permission.

Chapter 4

1. Zig Ziglar, *See You at the Top* (Gretna, Louisiana: Pelican, 1977), 118–119.

Chapter 5

1. Gary Smalley and John Trent, *The Blessing* (Nashville: Thomas Nelson, 1986), 61.

2. Lenning, *Blessing in Mosque and Mission*.

Chapter 7

1. Ziglar, *See You at the Top* 118–119.

Chapter 12

1. Frederick Wisloff, *Rest a While*. Originally published as *Hvil Eder Litt*, (Indremisjonsforlaget A.S., Oslo, Norway, 1948).

A PLACE FOR YOUR RESPONSE

List the names

of those you want

to encourage

with a blessing.

Tip: Begin with a simple phrase; add to it as your heart leads; use examples from the Scriptures.

Bless the Lord, O my soul,

And all that is within me, bless His holy name.

Bless the Lord, O my soul,

And forget none of His benefits;

Who pardons all your iniquities,

Who heals all your diseases;

Who redeems your life from the pit,

Who crowns you with lovingkindness and compassion;

Who satisfies your years with good things,

So that your youth is renewed like the eagle....

The Lord is compassionate and gracious,

Slow to anger and abounding in lovingkindness....

For as high as the heavens are above the earth,

So great is His lovingkindness toward those who fear Him.

As far as the east is from the west,

So far has He removed our transgressions from us.

Just as a father has compassion on his children,

So the Lord has compassion on those who fear Him....

The lovingkindness of the Lord is from

everlasting to everlasting on those who fear Him,

And His righteousness to children's children....

The Lord has established His throne in the heavens,

And His sovereignty rules over all....

Bless the Lord, all you works of His,

In all places of His dominion;

Bless the Lord, O my soul!

Encourage your own heart to open up to the blessings God the Father offers you.

Rolf Garborg began his ministry in the Christian Publishing industry in 1966 as a twenty-two-year-old missionary in Puerto Rico selling books door-to-door. That meager beginning evolved into the establishment of a successful Christian bookstore and distribution center on the island, as well as the founding of Editorial Betania, a Spanish publishing house that continues today.

Upon returning to the United States in 1975, Rolf continued in leadership for a variety of publishing organizations before cofounding Garborg's, a Christian gift company. When Garborg's was sold in 2001, he started Garborg & Associates, a consulting company serving the Christian publishing and gift industries. Rolf's career has taken him to all fifty states and nearly 100 countries, providing him the opportunity to bless and be blessed the world over.

Rolf has been married for more than forty-five years to Mary. They are blessed with two children and five grandchildren. Rolf and Mary currently reside in Minnesota.

Additional copies of *The Family Blessing* by Rolf Garborg are available from your local bookstore, or visit his Web site at: rolfgarborg.com.

FAMILY FAITH™ CELEBRATIONS

Maximize faith milestones with families.

Family Faith™ Celebrations are events celebrating the spiritual growth of children—from birth through high school. These faith milestones, like mile markers on the road map of spiritual formation, are moments a child or teenager publicly marks his or her journey with God.

Because these milestones are times families feel the need to celebrate, they're unique opportunities churches have to connect with and train parents.

First Bible—Marking the milestone when children receive their own copy of God's Word.

Families grow together in faith and with your church with these milestones...

Family Faith™ Celebrations offer more purpose and deeper spiritual growth through meaningful parent training. Each *Family Faith Celebrations* kit comes with parent training material on an interactive DVD featuring Dr. Brian Haynes, author of *Shift: What It Takes to Finally Reach Families Today,* so training will be fun for families and simple for church leaders!

Each *Family Faith Celebration* contains these important elements:

A Family Time Together training session—help families draw close to each other…your church…and God.

An All-Church Celebration—you can adapt or use as is.

An At-Home Celebration—a powerful, memorable time families can enjoy with friends and family in the intimacy of their homes.

Family Faith Growth—tools families can use on their faith journey.

Each of the six milestone resource kits includes:

- ■ 1 LEADER GUIDE
- ■ 1 MEDIA PACK
- ■ 1 PARENT GUIDE
- ■ 1 MILESTONE MEMORIES FRAME
- ■ 1 ALL ABOUT FAMILY FAITH CELEBRATIONS BOOKLET

OTHER *FAMILY FAITH™ CELEBRATIONS* MILESTONES IN THIS SERIES:

Baby Blessing	Faith Commitment	Preteen Passage	Commitment to Purity	High School Graduation

Baby Blessing—Marking the milestone when parents present their baby to God.

Faith Commitment—Marking the milestone when a child chooses Christ as Savior.

Preteen Passage—Marking the milestone when a preteen passes from childhood into adolescence.

Commitment to Purity—Marking the milestone when a teenager comes to purity for life.

High School Graduation—Marking the milestone when a teenager launches from high school.

For more information, go to **group.com** or visit your favorite Christian retailer!

Give your child the heart and skills for a lifelong friendship with Jesus!

Ten simple, do-them-at-home sessions help parents lead their elementary children into a deeper relationship with Jesus. Sessions include games & activities—each adaptable for children of different temperaments and interests. It's high-impact family ministry that draws children closer to Jesus— and God!

Order your copy of *Passing the Baton* today!

▶ ISBN 978-0-7644-3875-2
   $14.99 *In Canada $17.49*

For better or worse, children learn by watching their parents.

For more information:
Go to group.com or visit your favorite Christian retailer!